fabric
Formwork

Edited by
Alan Chandler and
Remo Pedreschi

RIBA ⊞ Publishing

Published by RIBA Publishing

15 Bonhill Street

London EC2P 2EA

ISBN 978 1 85946 284 3

Stock Code 61862

British Library Cataloguing in Publications Data
A catalogue record for this book is available from
the British Library.

Publisher: Steven Cross

Project Editor: Susan George

Copy Editor: Kate Reeves

Design and typesetting by Kneath Associates

Cover image by Dirk Lellau (transposed view)

Printed and bound by Cambridge University Press

RIBA Publishing is part of RIBA Enterprises Ltd

www.ribaenterprises.com

Fabric Formwork was published with the
support of the Concrete Centre, the University
of East London and Edinburgh University.

contents

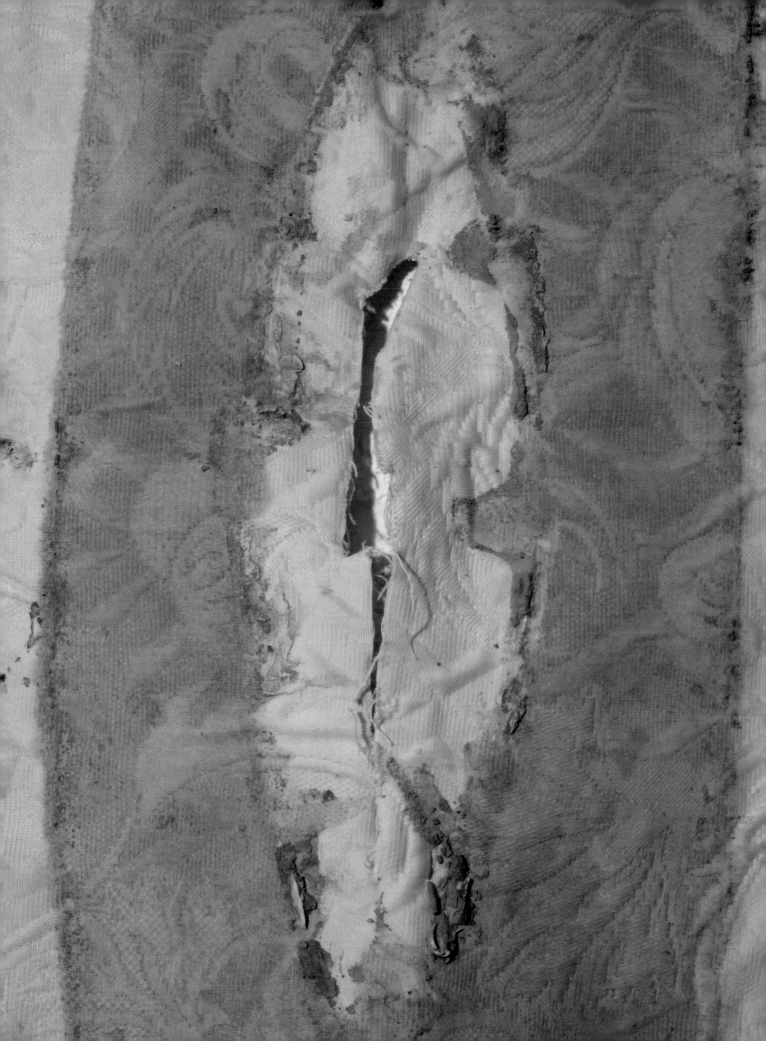

foreword

On a recent car ride with Remo Pedreschi at the wheel to an away-day of the University of Edinburgh and the Edinburgh College of Art the two of us got into an intimate and very animated discussion about concrete casting. I did not even realise how passionate I still can get about that. But in the eighties I spent years casting concrete (mostly black) in various forms for installations such as Apeiron in the Netherlands, or the Skin of the Earth in Moscow. This was work that forecast, metaphorically moulded, the long term urban project I am now involved in. Concrete has that capacity to move quickly from functional object to poetic model. Remo the structural engineer was as passionate, but about the casting work that is now happening in his laboratory in Edinburgh University and in the University of East London. We were like two birds in a dance above the beautiful Scottish hills, full of joy about this murky material that hurts your hands. I had seen by then the experiments he is conducting with students. But like this away-day that took place in these softly veiled hills and addressed the tricky issues of prototypical fusion projects between two schools, the formwork we discussed, shown here in this beautiful book

put together by Alan Chandler and Remo, is equally a fusion between the veils of fabric and the deep matter of the earth, and is quintessentially prototypical.

The research on fabric formwork pursued by the two universities, with the injections of workshops by Mark West, is beautiful, as the images here demonstrate, but also highly experimental and materially and conceptually challenging. It transfers the physical propensities of stretched fabric and its anthropomorphic characteristics and transforms these into the structural properties of fibre concrete. The result, an extremely seductive and surreal form language, mediates between the skin of the earth as a natural environment and the second skin of construction and inhabitation. This work intertwines the intuitive choreography of the hand that forms matter and the logical mind that constructs, assembles and imagines structural complexity.

Raoul Bunschoten
10 October 2007

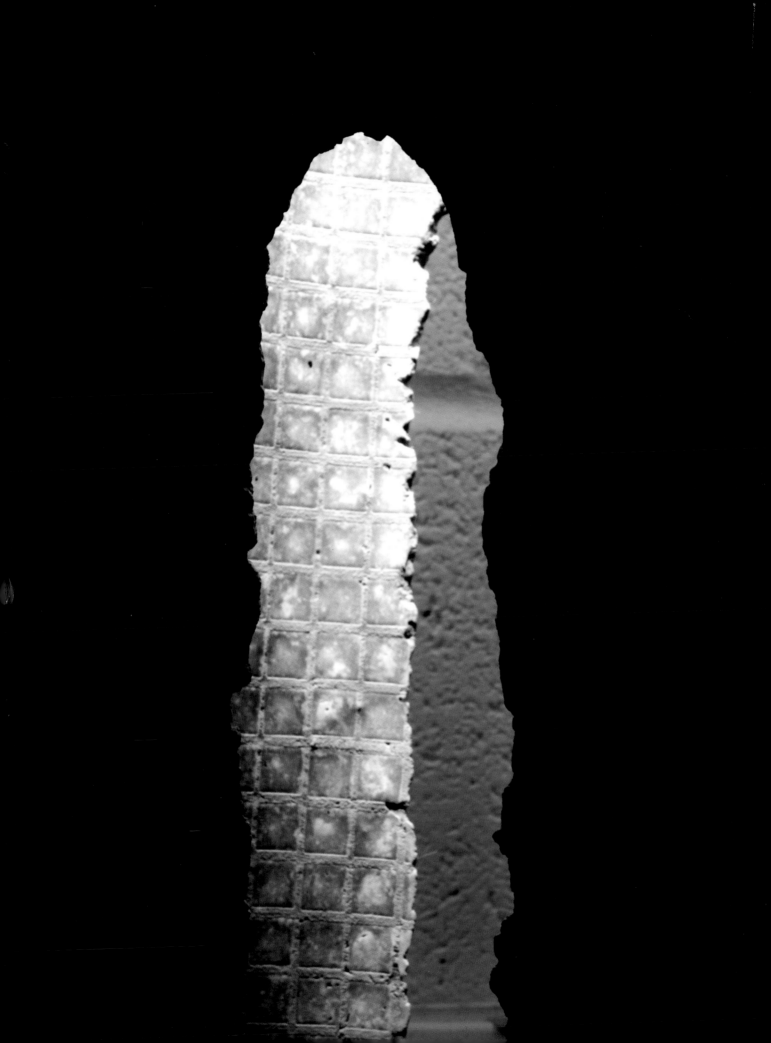

preface

Concretes are twenty-first century materials,[1] possessing metamorphic qualities demanded by modern construction and capable of being produced from a huge and increasing variety of recipes and methods of making. Close inspection of the fabric formed concrete pieces by Alan Chandler and Remo Pedreschi provokes an immediate response to the materiality of the pieces, which challenges Adrian Forty's theory that concrete is a process rather than a material. In these constructions the materiality is revealed as we engage in the form, structure, surface, colour and texture, and also sense the direct relationship between the makers and the making of these concrete artefacts.

'Hand built' is a mark of distinction, whether it applies to cars or clothing, and the reason for this is not hard to figure out – individuality, specificity and the connection to makers and their methods are attractive characteristics of bespoke products. At a time when a machine made world threatens to dominate every aspect of our existence, the demand for crafted artefacts remains high and Pedreschi's fabric forming process illustrates perfectly how concrete can be used in a way which responds to these demands (as shown in the fish bellied beam elements), and results in a product that can be reproduced with considerable accuracy.

Good architecture is relevant and connected to people and places through appropriate functionality coupled with an efficiency of means, where the whole possesses a psychological satisfaction. Fabric formed concrete provides relatively simple means to achieve individual solutions, employing forms with echoes of efficiency found in nature that achieve high levels of desirability.

The principal authors are to be congratulated on this publication which brings together two related research programmes and four supporting pieces which serve to locate and examine the work as becoming architecture.

The Concrete Centre is pleased to have been associated with the development of this research work from the early beginning and wishes the continued programmes at University of East London and Edinburgh University every success in the next stage of this exciting journey.

Allan Haines
Head of Education,
The Concrete Centre, September 2007

1.
The ability to transform a wide range of waste, recycled and organic materials into useful building materials for structural and non structural building elements. Examples of materials used to date: fly ash, blast furnace slag, recycled concrete, glass, plastics, shredded car tyres, waste ceramic and clay products, hemp, bamboo, rice husks and according to David Bennett, Concrete Consultant, certain kinds of confectionary.

introduction

The work described in this book is the product of collaboration: of ideas, attitudes and philosophy. It further represents a genuine and continuing collaboration between the schools of architecture at two quite different academic institutions: the University of Edinburgh, one of the four ancient universities of Scotland, and the University of East London, a new Docklands university in the Thames Gateway, one of the largest urban development areas in Europe. The strengths and traditions of both institutions can be easily seen in the projects described herein. A combination of academic rigour and creative endeavour, with paradoxically neither institution dominating in either field. The genesis of the collaboration helps to explain the background and underlying interest in a series of fabric formed concrete studies that forms the basis for this work. A shared interest in Eladio Dieste, the Uruguayan engineer, whose work sought for what he called 'Cosmic economy', led to an initial collaboration in the construction of one of his structures at UEL. There are many similarities in the underlying rationale of Dieste's work that are suggested by the use of fabric as formwork for concrete: the economy of means and materials, the use of structure as surface, the aesthetic of the doubly curved surface and perhaps more importantly, that

which may appear irrational being deeply rational. As an engineer and as a contractor, Dieste owned the risk of his ideas working, therefore achieving the apparently improbable through physical means. This mode of working has inspired the projects described here: setting broad criteria and then allowing the technology and design to evolve through the process of making.

As Schools, we are responsive to the ideas and innovations of the students who participate in the research. In 2002 Julia Hartmann at UEL and Francesca Crosby at Edinburgh both began experimenting with fabric formwork, drawing inspiration from the work of Mark West at the Centre for Architectural and Structural Technology (CAST) in the University of Manitoba. Shared interests in expressive economy and the value placed on constructive process led to a natural collaboration between UEL, EU and CAST, extending a shared interest in Dieste's work to the elaboration of new areas of fabric formwork investigation. This led to a joint invitation from both institutions to Mark West to be involved in workshop projects based on the theme of fabric cast concrete. The success of these initial projects opened up a large well of potential ideas to be drawn from, ideas that sought to expand the vocabulary of the process and challenge the limits of the technique, and that were complementary to the work of CAST. The template was then set for further projects. Different approaches were adopted to cover a range of objectives, with each institution contributing to the other's programme in a series of reviews and reflective studies. What is common to both is a shared attitude, a commitment to cross-disciplinary working and a desire to research through 'creative play'. Creative play is the process that Heinz Isler describes to develop an almost limitless variety of free-form shells whose geometry could not be readily defined mathematically, but which were nevertheless structurally correct, efficient and pragmatic. The rewards for mastering non orthogonal, 'natural' structures are huge, but require a new mindset – physical making now setting the agenda for analytical research, not the other way around. The improbability of taming, restraining and accurately controlling a mass of liquid concrete with a textile membrane becomes a technique with multiple advantages, acting as an effective critique of conventional methods of building, working with natural forces rather than expending energy and material suppressing those forces. Indeed one only has to refer to Nervi (1956) for an opinion on conventional casting techniques:

It may be noted that although reinforced concrete has been used for over a hundred years and with increasing interest during the last few decades, few of its properties and potentialities have been fully exploited thus far. Apart from the unconquerable inertia of our minds, which do not seem able to adopt freely new ideas, the main cause of this delay is a trivial technicality: the need to prepare wooden forms. (Nervi 1994)

Visitors to both institutions have a common reaction to the work. They are drawn immediately to the sensuous qualities of the concrete: the surfaces, the textures, the contours. When the process is explained, and furthermore that the farms were constructed by inexperienced students, then the sense of, as Dieste would put it, cosmic economy becomes apparent. To paraphrase Mark West, 'they get it'.

The general level of interest in the work has encouraged the creation of this book, whose aims are to present the work to date and to provide a critique from a number of contrasting positions. The six essays explain the nature of the research in different ways, considering practice and theory, aesthetics and the pragmatic.

The first two chapters by Alan Chandler and Remo Pedreschi are intended as a review of the work to date. Chandler describes the development of the work at the University of East London within the context of 'emergent' architecture, and elaborates on the nature of the prototype. Pedreschi then reviews the work at the University of Edinburgh, discussing the nature of the dialogue between the process of construction and the development of form, considering the control of the geometry needed to ensure the connection between the elements.

The next two chapters present contrasting viewpoints from the position of the practitioner and the theorist. Fiona McLachlan tells the story from the position of the practising architect designing fabric cast components in a project for social housing, in the first application in the United Kingdom of the technique, where neither the builders nor the consultants had any prior experience of fabric cast concrete. The process of design and adaptation from prototype to installation is analysed. Katie Lloyd Thomas uses the projects at East London to explore the theoretical implications for the architect allowing material to participate in its own form, and the issues of control and authorship that arise from this.

The final two chapters again provide a contrast between the aesthetic and the pragmatic qualities of the technique. Ilona Hay discusses the nature of the forms produced by the surfaces, establishing a set of criteria which condition our responses to fabric cast concrete. Daniel Lee, a PhD student currently researching fabric formwork, provides a review of the technical benefits of the casting techniques themselves.

The projects themselves have taken much from and given much back to the senior architectural students at both institutions. Using contemporary jargon the learning outcomes are manifest not only in the benefits of 'learning by doing' but also by the reflection on the processes, by the documentation and by the re-evaluation of the finished work. To this end the contribution of the architect and photographer Colin Fraser Wishart as tutor has been considerable and can be seen in many of the photographs in the publication.

Thanks are also due to the technicians at both institutions: Alastair Craig and Alan Ramsay at EU and Raphael Lee at UEL. The contribution of the workshop staff is direct to the ethos of both schools – a creative approach to making.

We are grateful also to Allan Haines of The Concrete Centre for providing support and encouragement for this publication, and to Messrs Don and Low for providing copious quantities of their most excellent fabrics. The senior students at both universities have been a delight to work with. Their energy, enthusiasm and creativity has been a powerful tonic for the tutor. It is not practical to name here but to each one we are grateful for the involvement. The final thanks are reserved for Mark West for opening our eyes to the potential of this work and for his enthusiasm and generous encouragement to pursue the particular paths we have chosen.

Alan Chandler and Remo Pedreschi

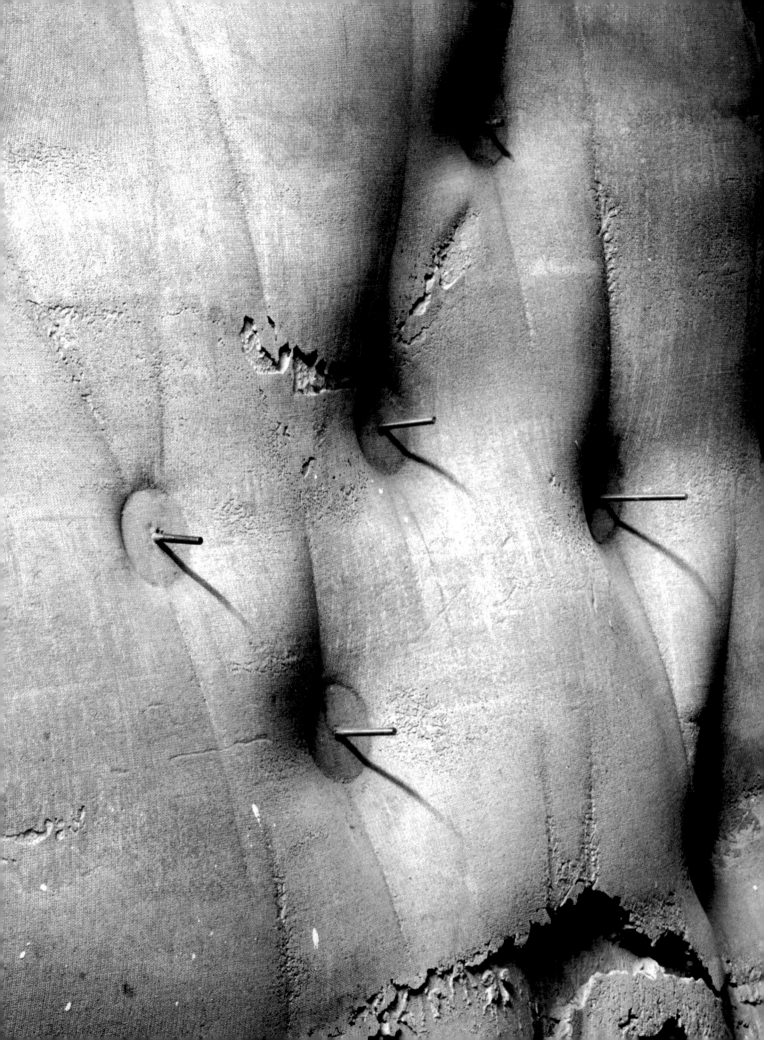

concrete as equipment

Alan Chandler

The use of fluid responsive formwork is a technique of constructing which allows the behaviour of material to engage with and influence the building process itself.

If the interaction of material and technique are allowed to influence the resultant form and performance, then the entire decision making process within the construction sequence comes under scrutiny.

This chapter explores the nature of architectural research through the fabric formwork research programme at the University of East London and the University of Edinburgh, and its role in the critical re-evaluation of the construction of architecture. Through the reinvention of the casting discipline, concrete becomes capable of new levels of formal and technical manipulation – capable of technical, intellectual and emotional refinement as equipment, with all the specificity of purpose that the term implies.

Fig 1

The 'Wall One' project sought to address the embodied energy issues of the concrete itself through the specification of recycled, manufactured aggregate. A partner in the workshop research programme at UEL is the MARC programme, based in the School of Computing and Technology. Under the direction of Darryl Newport the MARC programme, funded by the ENTRUST Landfill Tax Credit Scheme, recycles industrial waste, reclaimed granular material and organic sewage residues to create aggregates with specifiable size, density and colour. This 'smart' aggregate uses selected and metered dry powder resource material which is mixed at 1450 rpm, then mechanically pelletised using minimal water content.

As with the constituent mix, the size of pellets is also specifiable. Following the drying of the green pellets, they are heated in a trefoil kiln to vitrify the pellet surface, using the combustible potential of the organic matter in the blend to generate an internal honeycomb within each pellet. The greater the internal void, the lighter the aggregate, and owing to Wall One being situated within the main AVA building at UEL, cast onto the existing floor slab, it was the lightest specification, containing waste paper sludge, which was chosen. Further recycled materials were incorporated within the Wall in the form of shredded recycled plastic to act as an anti-crack reinforcement that has the capacity to flow around the dynamic curved interior of the formwork.

Fabric formwork is a language developed as a consequence of a consideration of edges. It is the antithesis of De Stijl inspired modernism where interpenetrating planes frame an ambition for architectural form. When casting with fabric, the textile and the concrete combine to deliver surface and form, and it is the restraint and constraint of edges and pressure points that articulate the language. In this sense fabric casting is akin to vernacular forms of incremental construction – brick and stone that is able through pixellated assembly to articulate both surface depth and structural mass, not simply a surface pattern.

In pursuing the performative limits of the fabric through analogue, rather than digital, research it will be possible to understand the predictive behaviour of the textile, and open the possibility for digital specification according to computational criteria. Work at the Centre for Architectural and Structural Technology at the University of Manitoba (CAST) and Edinburgh has established both the repeatability and accuracy of form making and the re-usability of the fabric itself.

There is an ambition for the establishment of a dialogue between materiality and purpose through developing techniques that synthesise material and programmatic constraints. Establishing an economy of means allows for the resolution of multiple, often conflicting, criteria in effective, refined technique, re-establishing a material intelligence belonging to vernacular construction within contemporary, often compromised, conditions of building: modern concrete operating as both passive and active, structural and environmental material – concrete as equipment.

'Fabric formwork' is a research programme that seeks to establish techniques that address complex issues of technical production, risk management and advanced passive energy control, but also accept the legitimate responsibility to be comprehensible

and relevant to everyday construction and everyday use.

Innovators in fabric formwork looked for opportunities to develop a technique that has the capacity to re-establish the dynamic relationship between making and thinking. The establishment of this relationship has taken a number of directions for these innovators – for Felix Candela and Christopher Alexander fabric acted as a permanent shutter for parabolic shells to create dignified, economic single spans for a school and as vaulting as part of the pattern language for self build worker housing, both in Mexico. For Miguel Fisac flexible formwork was a catalyst for elaborate surface claddings, from restrained textural treatments to blatant exhibitionism in buildings ranging between a single studio to vast hotels. Latterly Mark West has developed clarity and precision in structural elements such as beams (Fig 3) and columns, utilising the 'give' of the fabric to achieve constructed bending moment diagrams, mastering a structural economy. As a technique, in the bringing together of lightweight, inexpensive tensile fabrics with dense, compressive materials such as concretes, earth and lime a dialogue of opposites is set up, and resolved through the play of complex fluid dynamics and equilibrium. The resolution of tensile and compressive forces induces behaviour that in itself provides a fertile territory for technical laboratory based investigation.

Financial economy, an expressive form language, structural economy and 'emergent' behaviour are inherent within the potential of fabric casting. This chapter seeks to determine that the real value of architectural research is to consciously deal not with some, but with all of these aspects within the field of investigation. In identifying a multiplicity of readings within the potential of a technique, the unique integrated structure of architectural thought has distinct operational advantages

Fig 2
Wall One top edge detail.

Fig 3
Load testing a fabric cast beam at the CAST facility, Canada.

Fig 4
The pressure of liquid concrete at the base of the fabric formwork of Wall One.

2   3

over the binary, 'black and white' approach of conventional scientific method, valuing instead 'the grey'. The science of research – the paring down of the issues and the incremental, monocular approach to technical development – easily denies the possibilities that intuition and tactile experience can bring to developing the act of building. In closing in on the measurable, the intangible and the political are easily excluded. The nemesis of medical research is the issue of ethics, the human emotional response to scientific possibility clouding the factual advance of technique. This situation must not be so for architectural research. To 'economy' and 'form' we will now consciously add 'ethics', addressing as part of the development of technique the disenfranchisement of people from processes which build the physical realm. The development of responsive formworks is a conscious attempt to recognise and actively deal with technical, social and poetic issues within the act of building, insistent that the implication of ethics needs to be inherent in the work of building.

This ethical dimension requires definition in order to establish validity. Fabric formwork clearly displays a contemporary concern with 'emergence' – plasticity, indeterminacy and formal behaviour arising out of material characteristics. The fabric formwork research programme is also a critique of emergence as a current practice, and through the construction of this research distinct and important overlapping concerns are developed, clarifying how a research practice founded in material engagement and an architectural understanding of relativity can critique and extend the relevance of emergent study into wider, more valuable social and poetic concerns.

Ostensibly, responsive formwork shares much with the now common currency of emergence. The use of a textile formwork that responds to the hydrostatic pressure of concrete sets up a condition whereby the fabric describes curves between restraints that are a direct result of the interaction of pressure and resistance. The dialogue of pressure and resistance creates surfaces that belong to the family of membrane research undertaken by Frei Otto, but is manifest in mass 'hydrostatic' structures that are distinct from lightweight 'pneu' or tensile systems. The family of fabric construction includes tensile membranes, pneumatic structures, hydrostatic fabric formwork and shells derived from membrane form finding. The points of divergence within this family should be noted: tensile membranes, the development of which is Frei Otto's primary legacy, utilise the fabric as a

tensile field within defined parameters yielding optimal form between fixed points. Here, the fabric has a self organisation, but requires manipulation to render the tensile field uniform. Pneumatic structures are air pressure vessels requiring precise tailoring to orchestrate forms ranging from pure domes to cartoon characters depending upon the pattern. The work of Heinz Isler typifies the use of fabric as form-finder, using catenary principles inverted to determine the geometry of pure compressive shells achieved in concrete – the formwork for which is highly complex but rigid. Here the fabric dictates form through its own behaviour, but elaborate and costly means are required to achieve the constructed full scale version. By contrast hydrostatic fabric formwork is both form-finder and formgiver.

The contribution made by the inherent properties and contingencies of the fabric and the concrete make fabric formwork a technique and a form making process that properly demonstrates emergent behaviour. It is ironic that the minimal surface, associated emphatically with cable-nets, gridshells and canopies, is actually far more important to a mass structure such as stone or concrete – saving self weight through optimum geometry is vital with massive construction. With lightweight structures snow or wind loads are often as great as the self weight, so dynamic load considerations are then more applicable. The use of textile as formwork actually begins to unite the properties of mass and surface, tension and compression in a new relationship. (Fig 4)

Emergence as a practice in architecture has a relatively new legitimacy (Hensel, Menges and Weinstock 2004), drawing from scientific disciplines where the self organisation of matter and processes has been studied with increasing accuracy as computational techniques have matured: 'the concept of self organisation has been used in biology and computer science for many years. The question for us was, can its interpretation as an architectural metaphor or as a model for solving engineering problems expand the process of generating spatial effects through material means?'

The potential for the research process itself to begin to affect and construct multiple outcomes, using digital tools to generate increasingly elaborate design mechanisms, is effectively a new formal territory for architectural research: 'Rather than fabricating a teleology of research, then conclusions and finally designs based on those conclusions, the work consisted of following an open ended series of paths leading to an accumulation of ideas' (Wu and Roe 2005).

4

1

The concept that the very act of measurement interrupts the state of that which is being measured, disabling the 'truth' of how it is recorded and understood.

2

Strauven cites the primary intellectual contributors to the concept of relativity as Blake, Mach, Bergson, Husserl and of course Einstein, all of whom undertook to develop tools to understand phenomena as dynamic fields, not linear cause and effect.

3

Cedric Price (Potteries Think-Belt project), Archigram (plug in City project), Constant Niewenhuys (New Babylon project), Bill Hillier (Space Syntax 1976), Gordon Pask (Cybernetics).

4

Paul Coates in discussion with the author, December 2006.

Emergence derives its open ended, path-work methodology from an understanding of the implications of relativity. The principle of relativity sets out the scientific confirmation that all frames of reference are wholly equivalent regardless of their states of motion. With the single, prioritised viewpoint now obsolete, it is the specific relation between observer and observed which maintains validity, this validity shifting when the viewpoint shifts, with even the gaze itself conditioning and altering the dynamics of the viewer/viewed relationship. From this shifting pattern of relations, emergence as an idea develops the mathematical and by extension formal consequences of algorithmic development, the shifts in meaning and value through a process able to generate formal extension. When allied to material performance or techniques of adjustable repetition, complex structures are possible. The relationship of part – or component – to the mathematically developed whole is genetic in its origin, so holding to the reciprocal nature of relativity. The chosen viewpoint in relation to the genetic modelling process gives a prime role to the 'designer' of the emergent form; however the mathematical fluctuations through the chain of computations and algorithmic progressions enhance the 'errors' and feedbacks to allow unexpected or self generated form to emerge. Drawing from sub atomic physics, where the influence of the means of measurement has to be mitigated through the calculus of probabilities, or the 'uncertainty principle' of Heisenberg,[1] this play of errors constitutes a gateway into radical form making.

As with all process based, scientifically inspired research, the framing of criteria and the ultimate application of the work have to be carefully realised so as to avoid problematic conditions which compromise the clarity of the outcome. Where the subject of the research is relatively un-contentious, this editing of context in order to clarify criteria is acceptable and inevitable; the issue is less comfortable however when the ultimate goal of that research is the human environment (there is the apocryphal story of the emergent architect noting with pride how his research had benefited hugely by removing the 'problematics of site and user'). The generation of a field of ideas from the elaboration of a single process immediately poses a question about how that field is critically appraised in order to refine the result, and what is eliminated in order to arrive at a reduced set of manageable criteria. In the study of biological or physical behaviour this is not a negative characteristic; in architectural discourse however this limitation has serious

implications for the relevance of the work to the community of interests that architecture serves. In order to question and expand the relevance of emergent research, the architectural potential of relational processes needs to be re-examined.

The most fascinating area of relativity is conspicuously absent from 'emergent' text and discussion to date – that relativity as a concept was developed by thinkers who commonly held an abhorrence of unilateral compulsion and hierarchy either politically, socially or scientifically, and therefore the relevance of relative concepts has obligations to confront those aspects of our lives, and not simply the formal aesthetic language of our surroundings.[2] Emergent behaviour ought to be self evident, a material fact that everyone can recognise and experience, not an exclusive domain of specialised intellectual and computational endeavour. The ethical question is not simply how far digital form generation can interact with digital production, but also how the actual, not assumed, computational behaviour of material under use can contribute to economic, social and political situations.

Ironically, there was a distinct radical agenda common to early emergent researchers,[3] for whom form was not the goal of computational potential. The anti author impulse was a characteristic of radical post-war architectural practice: 'for a short period, … it looked as is if an "other architecture" might indeed emerge, entirely free of the professional pre-conceptions and prejudices that have encrusted architecture since it became "an art"' (Banham 1966, p.134). Here Reyner Banham outlined the radicalism he sought in *The New Brutalism*, but the intention to efface the random subjective of architecture was embedded within the work of early emergent behaviour researchers, for whom the intention was to devise design processes with 'an ambition to create a new vernacular'.[4] Such work was anti mannerist, anti individualist, and with hindsight harboured almost Maoist concerns for collective egalitarianism without the privilege of 'the profession'. For architecture to truly re-invent itself, a means of determining the built environment had, according to Banham, to accept the notion that 'the relationship of parts and materials of a building are a working morality.

His assessment of the demise of this radical moment in modern architecture concerns what he believes to be architecture's inherent aestheticism, thwarting the development of a truly technological, and by extension digital, practice: 'every reformist trend in architecture, back through Adolf Loos and William Morris, and Carlo Lodi and Colin Campbell, is backward looking' (1966, p.135).

The valuable question for current emergent practice, which operates with a distinctively radical written and formal discourse, is to assess how far the current use of digital processes operates within the 'encrustation' of artistic ambition, or exceeds the formal and subjective impulse within the historical practice of architecture. The relationship of the will to the form has not been severed in current emergent practice. The idea of a 'new vernacular' implies a common currency of knowledge, material competence and shared values without hierarchy of production of ideas. It is the ownership of 'the idea' that truly constitutes an architecture of common currency, and that the avant-garde in architecture has always protected. In this sense, emergent architecture remains firmly within 'the profession', and through a continually shifting visually inventive output maintains the architect's traditional role as formal tastemaker.

It could be argued that 'vernacular' now resides in the DIY superstore, with its melange of solar powered water features, carbon fibre patio doors, SatNav wristwatches and LED chandeliers, the aesthetic idea belonging to tradition, rather than reinvention. To accept that architecture ought to develop a deeper awareness of how its production of ideas can interact with its end users, and how the users can begin to own the ideas of architecture, requires that the immediacy of material sensation, simplicity of technique and practical sustainability are the focus of invention and attention, not the generation of form.

Architectural form is inevitably predetermined by the medium of graphic, not tectonic, expression. Despite procedural differences and formal preoccupations, there is little to distinguish between the classicist's pen and ink wash and the digitally derived model as a basis for building – both outputs are material-less, and must be passed to the master mason or CNC machine to duplicate, in either stone or styrofoam formwork. The severance of architectural conception and material engagement is the same, the practice of architecture less about intention, more about translation, with materials used because they are the nearest to the rendering, rather than because of a more holistic, generous set of considerations. What is at stake is integrity.

The fabric formwork research programme presents its inherent familiarity, ease of

manipulation, economy and availability as an egalitarian starting point. The interaction between its own textile nature, its support and organisation according to need and necessity, and the characteristics of the material – be that earth, cement or lime based concretes – sets up a dynamic relativity that needs to be worked through on the ground before the digital becomes relevant. Relativity is an immensely fertile concept, elaborated by Aldo Van Eyck in architectural terms through intellectual and architectural explorations of the 'in-between' (see Strauven 1998). In fully embracing the tactile, emotional role of the observer – or maker – within the process of production, the social and political agenda of Einstein, Mach and other originators of relativity can be reinvested. The physical expression of relativity through material interaction with the maker is reintroduced into the process, which as a whole is understandable, provable and focussed, yet in its detail can respond to local conditions, specific emergent phenomena, and emotional intervention. It is worth recounting how the structural engineers at Buro Happold used software to determine the thickness of timber in the development of the 'gridshell' structure at Windsor Great Park in 2005, only to be told by the carpenter contractor that wood that thick does not bend. The engineers then constructed 1:5 timber models to adjust the software.[5]

The practice of form manipulation through computational processes demonstrates a clear tendency to treat material as inert, a simple recipient of imposed form. The question is how far factors of safety or formal preoccupation enhance or mask the physical work that materials undertake within architectural construction. Material practice does not need to be predicated on overt materiality. A material's properties of stiffness, texture, strength or colour can be rendered mute, suppressed or exacerbated according to the wider matrix of responsibilities that the architecture adopts. It is the conscious understanding of the choices that are made in elaborating architectural proposals which is required, the limitations as well as the possibilities of an intellectual process dealt with critically.

Emergent phenomena cannot be reduced to formal and structural concerns alone without risking a separation from the core purpose of architecture, which is the construction of social relations. The fabric formwork project consciously addresses wider architectural interests in the development of its research agenda.

5
Jonathan Royons in discussion with the author, March 2006.

3-way relativity –
the poetic, social and economic

If architecture is to actively deal with a matrix of possibilities and responsibilities, the relativity principle, which Van Eyck began to appropriate for the discipline, needs to inform how material, spatial and social construction is conceived, elaborated and used. The poetic, the social and the economic are not peripheral to architectural research; they are core within the elaborate matrix, and their constant redefinition and circumstances are as follows.

Poetics

Beyond [concrete's] mythology as a machine age material lies the wish for its construction to be responsive to its inherent qualities – its ability to run and slump, its weight. No matter how precise and rigid the formwork, it always deflects as the material is poured and settled. If only that deflection could be worked with a skilled eye, the bowing of the wall as an imprint of the formwork would not have to be disguised, it could take part in the spatial dynamics of the building. (Salter 1989, p.62)

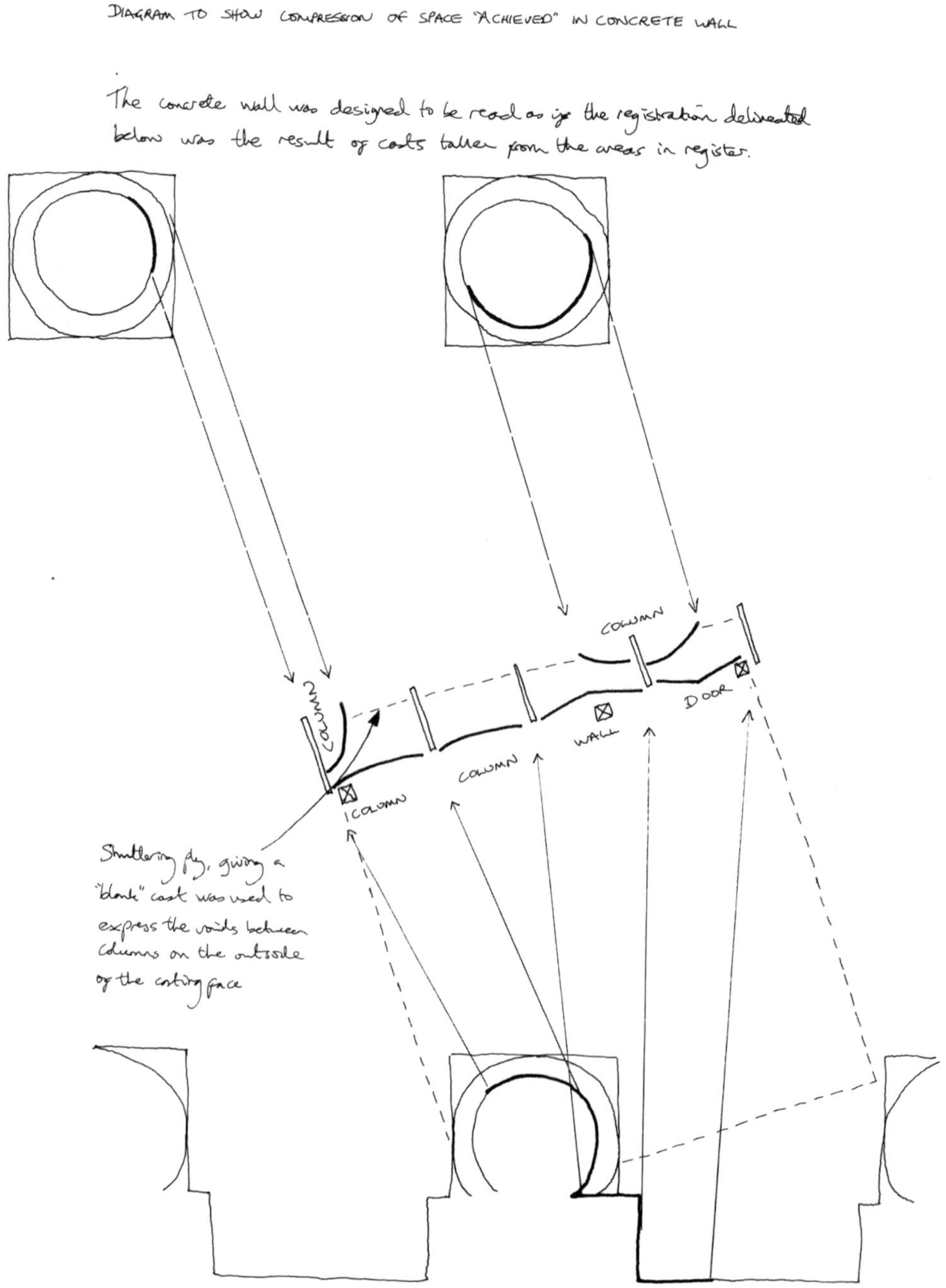

DIAGRAM TO SHOW COMPRESSION OF SPACE "ACHIEVED" IN CONCRETE WALL

The concrete wall was designed to be read as if the registration delineated below was the result of casts taken from the areas in register.

COLUMN

COLUMN

WALL

DOOR

COLUMN

COLUMN

COLUMN

Shuttering ply, giving a "blank" cast was used to express the voids between columns on the outside of the casting face

Fig 5
Diagram to show compression of space to be achieved in the concrete wall

G1

An essential characteristic of poetry is that it can elaborate an understanding of the passing of time and the inscription of the human condition within material or spatial circumstances. What Salter is discussing is the opportunity inherent in technical processes for the discovery and articulation of a human response within a constructed materiality. Articulated by Le Corbusier as 'Beton Brut', the tactility and apparent nature of the rough work was elevated beyond the immediate 'disadvantage' of imperfection to an appreciation of the revelation of the process of construction, its textural qualities in light, and its advantages of economy. The use of fabric is similarly frank in its expression, and similarly challenging to the received notions of the perfect construction and 'building as product'.

The poetics of deformative casting was in response to a research project instigated with great foresight by Michael Weinstock at the Architectural Association in the early 1990's (fig 5,6,7). Hessian, bitumen and paper pulp was used as a means of recording, reproducing and through the results flexible

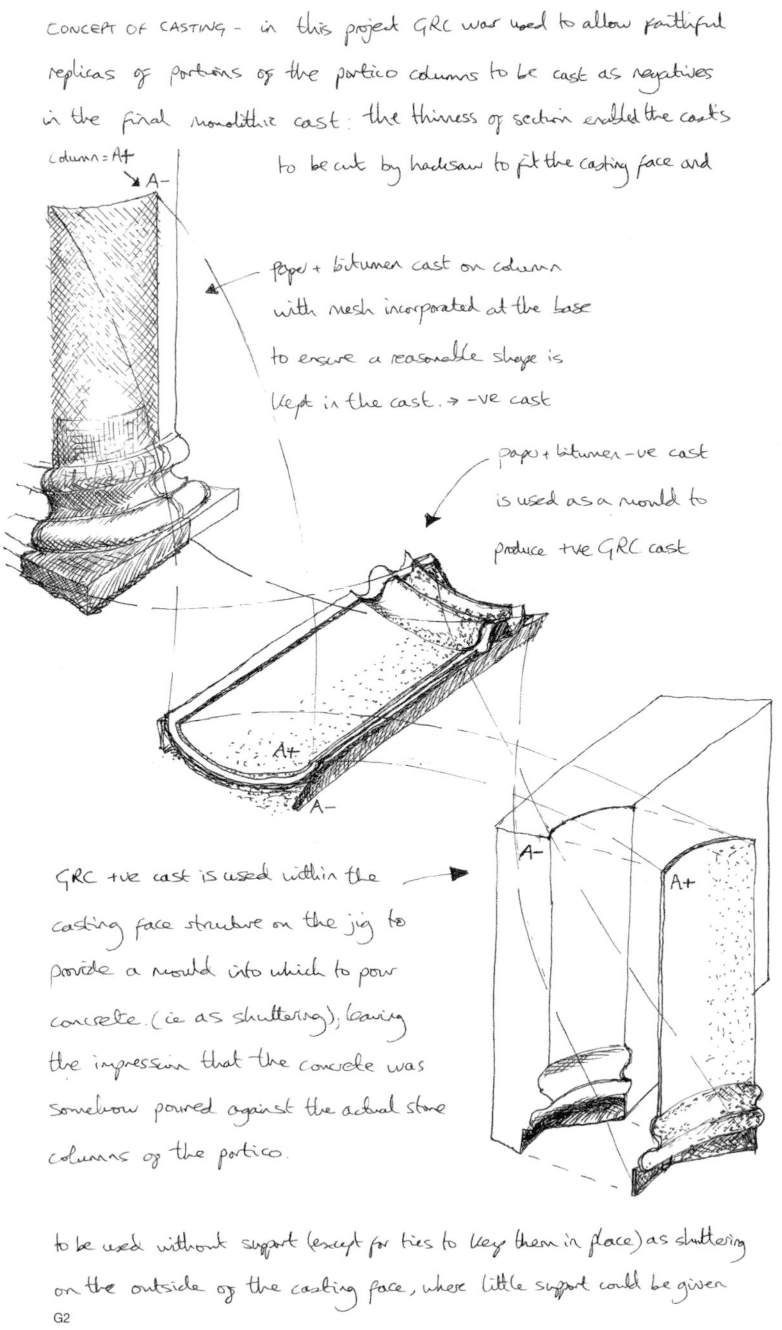

CONCEPT OF CASTING - in this project GRC was used to allow faithful replicas of portions of the portico columns to be cast as negatives in the final monolithic cast: the thinness of section enabled the casts to be cut by hacksaw to fit the casting face and

column = A+

paper + bitumen cast on column with mesh incorporated at the base to ensure a reasonable shape is kept in the cast. → -ve cast

paper + bitumen -ve cast is used as a mould to produce +ve GRC cast

GRC +ve cast is used within the casting face structure on the jig to provide a mould into which to pour concrete (ie as shuttering); leaving the impression that the concrete was somehow poured against the actual stone columns of the portico.

to be used without support (except for ties to key them in place) as shuttering on the outside of the casting face, where little support could be given

G2

Fig 6
The paper and bitumen cast of the portico door and architrave, pierced by registration rods used to link the eight concrete panels as one piece. 'A flattening out of the deeply recessed façade of the church took place in the paper and bitumen due to its nature as a flexible material', Luisa Auletta.

SECTION THROUGH MOULDS

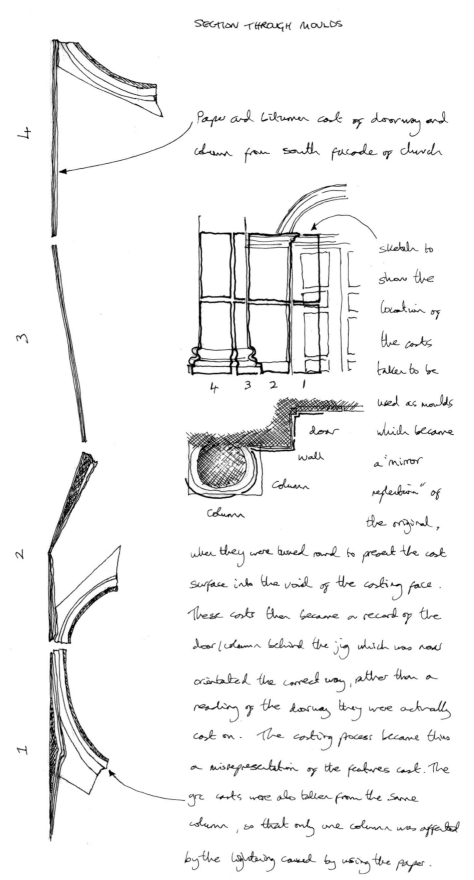

Paper and bitumen cast of doorway and column from south facade of church

sketch to show the location of the costs taken to be used as moulds which became a "mirror reflection" of the original, when they were turned round to present the cast surface into the void of the casting face. These casts then became a record of the door/column behind the jig which was now orientated the correct way, rather than a reading of the doorway they were actually cast on. The casting process became thus a misrepresentation of the features cast. The grc casts were also taken from the same column, so that only one column was affected by the lightening caused by using the paper.

door
wall
column
column

4   3   2   1

Fig 7
Horizontal section
through formwork
showing location of each
cast on the façade of St
Georges, Bloomsbury

formwork, manipulating the space via the casting process. Concerned with spatial effect and intellectual elaboration, the exercise more importantly allowed the process of construction and the evidence of decision making to become enfolded in the work, to have the action and therefore human presence intrinsic to the technical accomplishment. Rachel Whiteread's 'House' in Bow several years later posed similar questions, but was overwhelmingly about loss and a domestic poignancy of family space. Titled 'Editing the Total Room' (after a response to the work of Norwegian architect Sverre Fehn), the project was concerned more with establishing an intellectual protocol for casting, useful in the elaboration of future propositions – in that sense 'architecture' rather than 'art'. The 'Total Room' project aimed to realise in concrete a fictitious compression of space within the portico of the Nicholas Hawksmoor church 'St Georges', in Bloomsbury, London. Using the process of casting in a literal and metaphorical way, the duplication of 'real' surfaces into 'false' cast surfaces was a muse on how material and technique mediate ideas and ideals.

The act of duplication inevitably copies only some aspects of the original: how those aspects are selected, how the process of duplication itself begins to dictate the consequences beyond the initial intention, became the main purpose of the project. Respect for the listed stonework of the church led via experimentation to the use of 100 per cent cotton linter paper pulp as a vehicle for taking the registration of the surface, applied using a deckle as an appliqué from the papermaking technique. This was reinforced with layers of hot bitumen and hessian to

bind the cast together, and to allow the hydrostatic pressure of the final concrete cast to participate in the consequent final form through a controlled deformation.

The second face of the concrete – the free-standing columns of the portico – was converted from paper negative to a positive in glass fibre reinforced cement. Shuttering ply, which is the common parlance for concrete walling, was used to 'stand in' for the space between the columns – a conceptual flaw foisted on the work by the reality of creating a cast, and one which Whiteread's work also fails to overcome.

The paper left the stone unharmed, but ironically, and in a manner Heisenberg would appreciate, lifted from it the actual surface of accumulated soot and grime, depositing it onto the concrete cast. The fictitious compression of space actually presented the 'real' surface to the viewer. The idealisation of the concept is far richer when the 'ideal' is not fixated on the result, but on the rigour of the process. To accommodate the inherent nature of a technique and a material allows space for these elements to contribute to the work, to lend an authenticity to the result which, like vernacular architecture, achieves a form of humanity through its accumulated growth and sense of inevitability. The accidental, the circumstantial and the blemish are not weaknesses; they are aspects that are inherently human, and if handled intellectually become an advantage. In this project there is a belief that human presence in the physicality of the built work is important, that this readability creates a dialogue with the viewer or user, and that in some way this form of communication and empathy is an inherent quality of architectural expression.

Fig 8
The negative–positive casting sequence

Fig 9
The cast face – two of the three GRC panels are in place.

Fig 10
The first line of panels cast, the shuttering ply between the column casts can be seen.

Fig 11
Detail of the compressed space

8   9   10   11

6

Extract from 'Manifesto: Jig', unpublished study by Luisa Auletta and Alan Chandler.

We define the act of making as a constitution through improvisation with found objects and materials. The architectural process as event, responsive to the accident and implication of juxtaposing materials and objects, the act of making and use. Assemblage is the wilful manipulation of both associations with materials and of the reading of the history of events within objects, allowing the incident of construction to generate its own references. Adjustment is inherent within assemblage and is the means by which these disparate associations are combined. The result of

physical adjustment – informed by intention – is a re-inscription of the meaning deduced between proximate objects providing new fields of resonance.[6]

Fabric formwork actively incorporates the direct actions of its makers upon the material being worked. A challenge in developing construction techniques with the required thresholds of safety and predictability is that the spontaneous and the contingent become edited out of the activity. With much of architectural production focussed on one-off

12

13

14

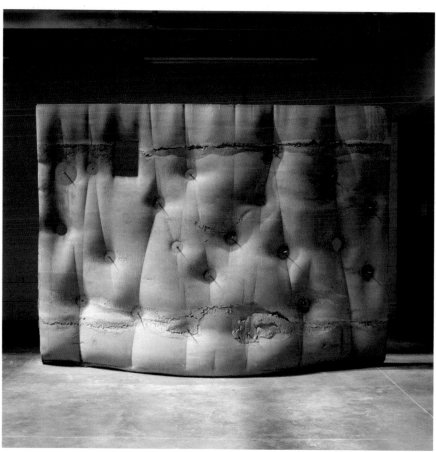

Fig 12,13,14,15

sequence of construction Wall One

15

buildings for particular users and locations, it is key to address the issues surrounding bespoke production, of architects being equipped to exercise judgement and dexterity both at the design stage and production stage of building. David Pye, in his book *The Nature and Art of Workmanship*, makes a distinction between the 'workmanship of risk' and the 'workmanship of certainty'. He clarifies the role of the individual maker with regard to either being involved with the determination of the result, or being placed outside a predetermined mechanical (or digital) process. Clearly the 'workmanship of risk' reflects the ambiguities surrounding the reality of architectural practice, to quote: 'In the workmanship of risk, the result of every operation during production is determined by the workman as he works and its outcome depends wholly or largely on his care, judgement and dexterity' (1968, p63). In other words, can one determine the accuracy of a built result more confidently by using techniques that do not prescribe the outcome entirely, but rather incorporate adjustment and judgement within their operation?

The frame for 'Wall One' was an elaboration of the idea of a jig, developing the term as a device for holding a piece to be worked in dialogue with the piece, not simply a means of predetermining and re-producing that piece exactly (as with conventional shuttering). This is an important distinction, if the relationship between the constructor and the material is to yield an element of the unforeseen and is a means of determining a systematic construction that retains a tactility of craft. In framing an activity, rather than predetermining it, a jig is a conceptually looser and more open ended mechanism than a simple formwork. Its precision lies in the clarity with which it enables a range of operations to happen. Casting is no longer a process of replication; rather it becomes, with the use of textile, a field of possible outcomes within a fixed set of parameters.

Social

On one hand, then, is a rich attitude linked by osmosis to the system's sophisticated tools and wealth of information, an attitude that imitates and mediates reality, that determines the dichotomy between art and life, public behaviour and private life. But contrary to this is a 'poor' inquiry that aims at achieving an identity between man and action, between man and behaviour and thus eliminates the two levels of existence.

Germano Celant, 'Arte Povera:
Note for a Guerilla War'
(in Christov-Bakargiev 1999)

It is therefore essential for an object and also for the world to present themselves to us as 'open' … and as always promising future perceptions.

Umberto Eco
'The Open Work' (in Christov-Bakargiev 1999)

16

17

The work of Christopher Alexander in developing processes of making architecture as a collective act is particularly relevant to the ambition of the fabric formwork programme. The invention of 'new vernacular' building techniques establishes a commonly held and understood pattern language which develops from the material engagement of participants, circumstance and material properties. Construction practice emerges from that interrelationship – a relativity of practice and the practice of relativity. Alexander's use of fabric formwork as part of the Mexicali development was one of many techniques which in their direct simplicity reinforced the project ambition for a common practice, adding an elevated, ambitious geometry to a rectilinear form language as vaulted connecting colonnades (1985, p.30).

The network of constraints and criteria which exists in actual constructed situations establishes a fertile ground for problem solving, the exercise creating in one event a series of follow up scenarios for investigation. With the interaction of details understood, the research can determine a sequence of follow up work that develops interaction to an optimum. Without that initial overview, the strategic clarity is absent, and the interaction of elements is unexplored. There is clearly huge potential in the computational elaboration of ideas, but it is suggested as part of a wider matrix of research that is purpose driven, and in its elaboration maintains the working morality alluded to by Reyner Banham.

The drawing and its abstraction normally precede the making of structures with material. Within the Workshop, this is not so, and the line loses its pre-eminence. Workshops rely on both verbal and manual exchange in order to generate the constructed situation between the participants and their task. The architect should be taught not to assume that the mastery of matter in order to achieve form is always the responsibility of others. In the very conception of a design the qualities and properties of materials must be grasped and understood in order to make.

Knowledge acquisition and application can be embedded within the same activity. The concept that thinking is a singular and cerebral activity is actively countered by workshop practice. Jean Prouve's method of thinking through making engages the tactile fabricator in the act of refinement – his drawing board was adjacent to the metal press and allowed for the building of an idea before a drawing was made. This creates a situation whereby manual labour becomes valued in the creation of new form and function, with the interaction of material, structural performance, form and production technique addressed in one operation. The engagement of the manual and conceptual in the same moment embraces the value of fabricator and originator within the production of objects and architecture. The non-hierarchical, profit sharing workshop structure of Jean Prouve's manufacturing organisation reinforced the conviction that material progress can only be achieved by social progress. The context and structure of fabrication is rarely a factor in the elaboration of research; however within the discipline of architecture it is a valid consideration, and within the fabric formwork project informs the development of technique and application.

Economic

An economy of means is more from less, not simply same for less. The development of a material research culture needs to prioritise investigation that understands issues at a number of simultaneous levels. When examined from a sustainable perspective, the economy of highly engineered and materially efficient components may achieve low monetary unit costs but may never pay back the energy investment made in their manufacture, and may be so lean of purpose as to be redundant for future re-use or adaptation. Material research has to deal with future potentials as well as current economic imperatives, and there are clear advantages to developing lean techniques rather than lean products. The materiality of vernacular building traditions not only offers us economically derived, circumstance specific architectural responses, but leaves a rich material legacy or reservoir for future use, re-use or adaptation. It is often a material abundance that allows environmental, structural and cultural advantage to co-exist within buildings. This unitary conception of 'vernacular' can be applied to non-derivative research, with the fabric formwork research consciously working towards solutions that deliver simultaneous advantages – thermal mass, acoustic specificity, efficient construction processes and carbon sinks utilising recycled or carbon rich waste as constituent materials. (Fig 18) Formal economy is not by definition always financial or sustainable economy, and the advantages of emergent material behaviour can find expression in broader and more diverse areas than simply intricate geometry.

The structural clarity and simplicity of the Crown Hall at MIT by Ludwig Mies van de Rohe achieves its 'truth' and 'simplicity' through the downplaying of the 'truth' of

Fig 18
Research into the performance of fabric formwork with pneumatically rammed earth construction at UEL, 2005

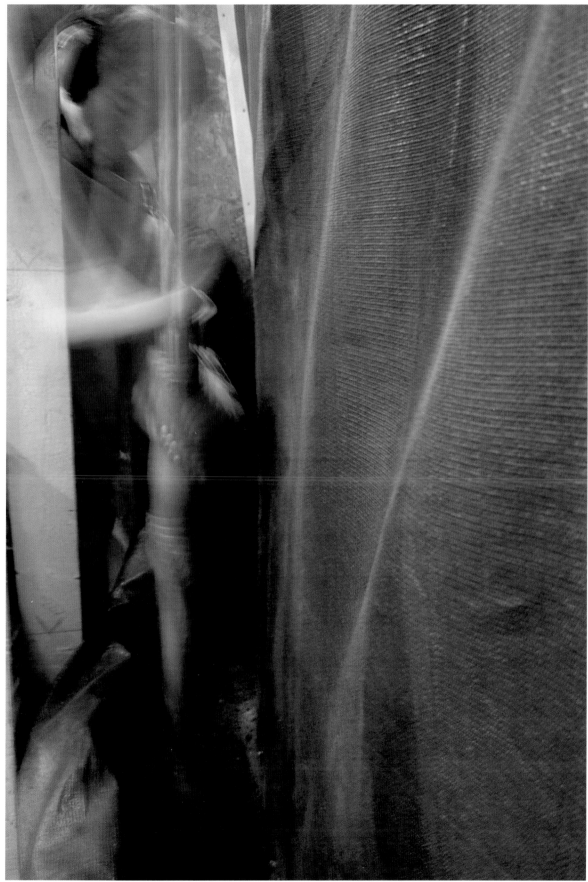

the bending moment diagram, thereby elevating the status of the fact of industrial production. The 'I beam' maintains a consistent depth from bearing to mid-span owing to its extrusion-like manufacture on a rolling mill, thereby wasting its own weight in non-structural material. In addition the external placement of the roof beams expresses their iconic, industrial significance but invites atmospheric attack to a reckless degree. Here the logic of an undifferentiated industrial production (of steel) and the desire for expression (of industry as art form) clearly overrides the logic of natural structural economy, and it is precisely this interaction of production, material performance and formal preoccupation which actually expresses the true field of ideas which architectural processes need to negotiate. The same pre-occupation with a logic of formal and iconic expression to the detriment of actual logical construction could equally be applied to architectural form generated from the skin of a custard apple, where digital elaboration delivers a superabundance of form requiring correspondingly highly developed techniques of production and energy inputs to become realised as surface active architecture. If one understands Otto's reservations about the application of form finding to buildings, where for him such 'work can only be seen in relationship to the complexity of a building task and the integration of the building into its surroundings and into society' (1990, p.5), the counter to this might be to employ lean techniques that deliver a generosity of performance. Fabric formwork is one means of achieving such a technique, having distinct advantages in producing concrete over rigid formwork, chiefly in its responsiveness and adaptability during the pour through a readability of the liquid concrete's behaviour.

The jig to hold the textile and to allow it to remain responsive must be designed to minimise material use: in developed economies to minimise the unnecessary production of carbon, in developing economies as a response to a potentially restricted 'economy of means'. An interest in Buckminster-Fuller's notion of 'tensegrity' as the resolution of forces within the structure itself, converting dynamic loads into dead weight, informed the research into the opposition of cables and tension props resisting the fluid concrete weight and fabric deformation. The use of rigs to transfer the downward pull of the concrete onto the upward thrust of acro props via cabling uses tensile containment where possible in preference to wholly compressive elements

of containment – limiting the formwork weight wherever possible. Side panels can define precise vertical edges to a cast, allowing it to be continued in sections to create the whole. The constructional variety available through the use of the catenary nature of pressure structures is both a structural advantage (greater endurance for less material), and formally liberating.

Techniques for casting walls and beams are now empirically established. The extension of fabric formwork research into structural, thermal and acoustically active structural slabs commenced in 2006–7. This area of research seeks to minimise the potential dead weight of concrete as it swells below the horizontal datum of the reinforcement. The proven use of sleeved, grouted tendons which can follow the major undulations of the slab, set at metre centres, significantly reduces steel use, and with the fabric's ability to create high points within the underside of the slab, thicknesses and weight of material between the major undulations (acting as beams) reinterprets the waffle slab not as a repetitious grid but as a variable field of datum levels – the fabric forming a connective terrain. The advantages of this form of construction are multiple: reinforcement can be minimised; materially concrete can be minimised; acoustically a full scale surface can be achieved which corresponds to a required sound modulation developed digitally or through models; thermally the surface area for absorption of heat can be enlarged without compromising weight or setting up undesirable acoustic conditions; services, including fibre optics, can be accommodated; visually the soffit can be a surface open to the designer's ambition. This multiple efficiency goes some way to establishing concrete as 'equipment'.

Establishing architecture as a material culture

The practice of prototyping is a proper domain for architectural research. Constructive processes and material inertia need to be thought of not as impediments to formal invention, but rather as active participants in innovation. As educators and as architects, the compulsion should be to build, learn and build again, a mode of operation at odds with traditional, non-architectural research practice. Conventionally a discrete series of operations would be defined which, through systematic and linear processes, became understood and evaluated according to pre-set criteria. Building at 1:1, informed with a limited but effective body of intuition and understanding, provides a broad platform from which significant areas of study – materiality, of process, of technique, can be tested simultaneously. It is only after the prototype is built that the scientific model of analysis becomes vital in refining the opportunities that full scale making has generated. The prototype tests the interaction of materials and events, not merely their constituent parts. In building a prototype, one discovers how to build, and where to focus the activity of risk, the value of team consciousness, and the consequences of theoretical decision making.

The nature of the architectural prototype is that it can act as an anticipation of the end of a process of thought. Simultaneously it is an enactment of that process. The power of a prototype is its ability to embody a field of ideas and the means of testing the interrelationship of those ideas in a single moment. A prototype accelerates the proposition.

Meaningful form is the result of thoughtful, disciplined integration of the written and the improvised. The reinvigoration of a practice, be it the jazz of Miles Davis or advancing architectural construction, has to question any singularity of approach, and to recognise the variables inherent in each different situation in order to devise strategies that, through the interplay of conflicting concerns, create new coherence.

Developing thematic concerns and work through a clear structure allows for a succession of improvisations: 'the building process … is a culture: a system of rules, and knowledge, and processes which spreads by word of mouth and hand to hand practice' (Alexander 1985, p.347).

The aim of re-examining the nature of architectural production through the fabric formwork research programme is to clarify the unique responsibilities that architecture possesses, and through example to demand that social, political, material and technical obligations which the practice of architecture works with are both informed and enriched by our collective effort.

dialogues in process and form

studies in fabric cast concrete
Remo Pedreschi

Even the most convincing techniques
of representation do not correspond fully
to the experience of the built reality.
Picon 2004, pp.114–121

Introduction

Trying to describe the idea of fabric formwork to cast concrete without the use of an image or example could possibly result in mild amusement, but almost certainly in mis-understanding. The use of fabric formwork, as the studies in this chapter endeavour to illustrate, is a viable, practical and expressive construction technique that raises questions about what informs the nature and the experience of material and process.

Materials that form buildings can be classified in many ways, depending on the point of view. A chemist or a scientist, thinking about materials, may consider the order of materials in terms of atomic structure; for example the structures that separate metals from polymers. The technologist is more concerned with properties at a macro-scale and how these might control the application and the utility of materials, the physical characteristics that determine strength and stiffness. The builder is concerned with process. Imagine the stone mason as he studies a piece of stone, considering the best way to work it, being more concerned about the manner in which its geological history influences the way it can be cut, dressed and used. The perception of a material, its materiality, in building and architecture, is continually under discussion. What are the intrinsic characteristics that inform its utility, process and expression? 'Materials derive neither from nature alone nor from mere progress in science and technology' (Picon 2006). The question posed by these studies in fabric cast concrete is at the heart of what the intrinsic material nature of concrete is. The question itself is, to a large extent, conditioned by viewing position. In education and research it is particularly important to bear in mind these viewing positions and to re-evaluate and re-appropriate the objects that are created from different perspectives. The true sense of a material comes from the ability of the observer to understand its nature from a series of different perspectives. Jean Prouvé understood this and expressed exasperation at both architects and engineers when they studied his work:

I noticed two things, one of these was the intense interest by technicians in the purely technical aspects of my projects, regardless of their content. The other was the equally intense interest shown by architects and users who saw in my projects an opportunity to modernise solely for appearances' sake (Huber and Steinegger 1971).

Designers and makers often approach the use of materials from different positions. The process used to form an object can be declared or denied. In some of the works of Calatrava for example, or the Guggenheim by Gehry, the process may be said to be denied; it is clearly the final form that controls the making and the means to construct are determined but not always influential. The form is not conditioned by its making. On the other hand it is clear that the work of Prouvé was heavily informed by the processes and materials available, with a close relationship between design and manufacture. The integration of process, materials and form is also seen throughout the works of Eladio Dieste. In many of his buildings there is a complexity of form, deliberately non-orthogonal, that at first may appear irrational but becomes truly rational when its form and construction process are understood: 'there can be no architecture without construction' (Dieste, Architecture and Construction 2004, pp.182–190).

All his buildings arise from the synthesis of structural form, its expressiveness, construction process and materials. The church at Atlantida can be appreciated and interpreted from these differing positions (Figure 1 (Pedreschi 2000)). The undulating surfaces of the wall and roof, if viewed from the position of the planar orthogonal orthodoxy associated with frame, may indeed appear irrational. However his buildings are actually very efficient structurally, simpler to construct than concrete and were built under conditions of severe economic stringency. Similarly many traditional forms of concrete construction have confused simplicity of form with rationality of process. The

temporary formwork often costs more than the material with which it is filled and form itself is conditioned by the means of making the formwork. The planar geometry of the formwork inevitably bends when resisting the pressure of the concrete and therefore requires substantial bracing to maintain its shape, to avoid leakage at the joints and to limit surface imperfections. Non-planar surfaces, following this process, are inherently more difficult and require more effort to make. When assessed against the orthodoxy of conventional formwork, non-orthogonal forms are immediately perceived as less practical. The use of fabric formwork suggests the opportunity to develop complexity of form using a rational process. Minimal use of material that requires minimal bracing, whose shape is dictated by its response to the forces it is intended to resist, will lead to a more expressive construction. To paraphrase Dieste, there is nothing more noble and elegant than to 'resist through form'. The studies in fabric cast concrete initiated by Mark West and CAST challenge the orthodoxies of concrete, where anything that deviates from the planar is regarded as complex, less rational and costly. The idea of fabric as formwork gains particular strength when seen from the position of conventional construction.

This chapter describes a series of studies that further develop the potential of fabric formwork and its inherent differences from more conventionally cast concrete. There is a great concern for the pragmatic and a particular consideration of this work is the nature of the connection between fabric cast concrete elements and a rationalisation of the processes needed to achieve the form and connection in a consistent and repeatable way.

Fig 1
The Church of Jesus
Christ the Worker,

Fig 2
Fabric concrete-twisted
form (R. Pedreschi)

1

2

In conventional construction, once concrete has been selected its form is often predetermined by the nature of the formwork. The doubly curved, hyperbolic paraboloid surfaces of Felix Candela were developed, to a large extent, by the need to make curved surfaces from planar material (see Faber 1963). Fabric formwork raises other challenges. How can the fabric be controlled to produce interesting surfaces while maintaining the inherent rationality of the process?

The process reveals a synergy between the fabric and the fresh concrete. The concrete gives shape to the fabric by its weight and then receives the form and surface the fabric produces in return. The research must deal with the dichotomy of form and process. Additionally we must reflect and continually refine the results, exploring the nature of the forms and surfaces given by the process. The research methodology requires a particular approach, somewhat different from empirically based methods most often associated with materials research, of isolating the variable and sequential analysis. It is one that endeavours to continually shift perspective between form and process, between expressiveness and rationality.

Methodology

Initial studies have revealed the beautiful forms and textures that can be produced with appropriate care and attention; however to fully understand the rational qualities the ideas have to be tested against practical issues such as accuracy of construction, repeatability and connection (Figure 2).

A series of projects was undertaken to consider the nature of the form and construction process. From these projects further strands of investigation have developed that study certain applications in much more detail. The studies were undertaken with senior architectural and engineering students of the University of Edinburgh. Through a series of seminars and demonstrations architecture students were exposed to the potential of the technique from a variety of perspectives:

> **form** – as appropriate architectural elements

> **process** – understanding appropriate techniques

> **surface** – the qualities of the form produced and its representation in terms of reflectivity and texture.

Working in small groups over a period of five weeks the architecture students were encouraged to experiment through a sequence of prototypes leading to the design and production at full scale of a series of objects with a clear architectural or building application. Important criteria were:

> rational use of fabric

> minimal use of materials

> consistency and control of the process

> the connection between elements.

Other projects were part of a broader research programme including post-graduate engineering students and academic staff. All the projects were carried out in the Architecture workshop at the University of Edinburgh.

Physically and chemically the concrete studied in this work is almost identical to conventional concrete.[1] Generally for the casts the same mix was used throughout, modified occasionally by using white cements or adding pigments.[2] No additives, for example plasticisers, were used.

Many different types of fabric were used including dressmaking cottons and polyester textiles. Various forms of geotextile fabric were also used. Geotextiles are strong, stiff and have good tear resistance. Virtually all the fabrics tested stripped easily from the hardened concrete.

Some fabrics with loosely woven yarns would leave traces on the concrete. Some dyed fabrics would leave colour traces on the concrete. Non-woven fabrics such as felts do not work so well and they can be difficult to strip.

Initially the studies focussed on generic architectural forms: beam, column, panel and wall. These terminologies gave direction to the studies. However a different classification developed more concerned with the process rather than the object produced. The classification relates to the interaction of the fabric and the concrete in its fresh or plastic state. The defining physical force in architecture is gravity. Gravity creates structure. Natural structures evolve that are conditioned by both their materials and the effect of gravity. Likewise the fresh concrete will generate downward, sideways and possibly upward pressure on formwork. Fabric can only resist these forces by tension and thus the form produced relies on controlling the reactions of the fabric to the forces produced by the concrete. Gravity then becomes a tool to be exploited in the generation of form rather than something that is resisted, as in conventional formwork systems. The overall geometry of the object is

1

In terms of mix proportions and materials used fabric cast concrete is identical to conventional concrete; however the permeability of the fabric alters the water content during casting, changing the hydration rate and curing regime and hence altering the properties of the hardened concrete; see Chapter 6.

2

Typical mix proportions were 10:5:4, aggregate (10 mm), sand and cement.

3

Spandex is a synthetic fibre with high elasticity. It is often used in sportswear and is known under various trade names such as Lycra.

3

4

determined by a patterning of the fabric and the arrangement of the formwork.

The surface can be further manipulated by careful stretching and pre-tensioning of the fabric prior to casting.

The projects have now taken place over three academic years. The results of each project are carefully documented and contribute to the brief for subsequent projects. The following results are broadly classified by their form although they are explained in terms of process.

Panels

These are the simplest to construct and provide a great opportunity to study surface and texture (Figure 3). Fabric is stretched across a normally rectangular frame onto which a second frame is attached. The second frame forms the edge of the panel. The assembly is suspended in a horizontal position (Figure 4). If concrete is cast onto the fabric at this stage a doubly curved surface running to the straight edged sides will be produced. The degree of curvature depends on the stiffness of the fabric and the pre-tension induced by stretching the fabric. Further tension can be induced by deforming the fabric upwards using projecting forms placed underneath the fabric, producing counter curvature to the surface. Many studies have been carried out using this technique.

It is also possible to manipulate the surface using multiple layers of fabric of varying stiffness. In one example a layer of stiff, geotextile fabric was stretched and a series of cuts was made in the fabric. A second layer of very flexible Spandex[3] was stretched over the geotextile (Figure 5).

The weight of the concrete causes the Spandex to be pushed through the geotextile

layer, creating additional relief on the surface of the panels. The friction between the two layers controls the deformation of the Spandex. The geotextile fabric creates a generally convex surface with pronounced lunette shaped convex ribs. The surfaces generated had a particularly appealing character and the process itself suggested further development to study the nature of convexity and concavity in concrete surfaces. As the panel is cast the form of the final surface becomes evident from the tension that develops in the fabric. New possibilities reveal themselves. The cast surface can then become the formwork for a second, concave panel, thus creating a reflection in relief of the first. The second panel also has a contrasting surface texture. The convex panel takes its texture from the Lycra whilst the concave panel takes its texture from the geotextile, except at the concave lunette depression.

The final stage in this process was to envisage the work as an assemblage of panels forming an undulating surface. Further panels were developed to articulate the surfaces around corners. The corner panels were twice the height of the original panels but were formed in a similar fashion, incorporating the ribs, but formed on a 90° curve. Inside and outside curves were formed, again by counter casting. The panels were assembled into an articulated, undulating façade (Figure 6).

By this stage the students had mastered the casting technique and were able to produce repeat casts of consistent quality and accuracy. A kit of parts had been developed which had interchangeable components that allowed many different arrangements to be prepared.

In another study the use of fabrics with variable permeability was considered. The fabric used was a rather gaudy dressmaking

Fig 3
Fabric cast panel (R.Pedreschi)

Fig 4
Casting panels (R. Pedreschi)

Fig 5
The combination of geotextile and Spandex (R. Pedreschi)

Fig 6
Undulating surface using cast and counter cast panels (R. Pedreschi)

5   6

7a

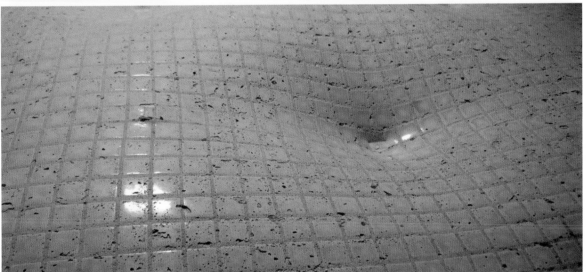

7b

material with a base of polyester or cotton. What is interesting about this fabric is the 1 cm squares of plastic film bonded to the fabric in a regular, orthogonal grid. The squares were separated by 2 mm joints. Concrete, when cast against plastic, produces a smooth glassy surface (Figure 7).

The results were surprising. A surface with the nature of mosaic crossed with a wire frame topography was found. The result is not simply a fortunate pastiche – the grid adds to the expression of the undulated surface quite differently from the experience of applied ceramics.

Beams

The work at CAST investigated linear elements cast horizontally. Such forms can be generated to produce structural beams

that are particularly expressive of the bending forces they are designed to carry. The projects at Edinburgh acknowledge these studies and have taken a different direction, resulting in quite different forms, driven by the following factors:

> repeatability and consistency of form
> connection to their parts of the building
> simplification of process
> understanding the structural behaviour
> optimising the form for structural efficiency.

One of the potential applications for fabric cast beams is in the production of pre-cast beam and slab systems. There is growing interest in using the thermal mass of concrete beams and slabs with exposed soffits to maximise the stored energy in the concrete. Needless to say where a soffit is exposed the quality of finish and expression of the concrete

Fig 7
Variable permeability
fabric (a) fabric, (b)
concrete cast from fabric

8

Fig 8
Initial prototype beam
(M. West)

becomes particularly important. The web can be shaped to follow the curve of the bending moment diagram, leading to a 30–40 per cent reduction in the weight of the concrete compared with an equivalent rectangular beam. If reinforcement follows the geometry of the bending moment then the total quantity of steel can also be reduced. An initial study was undertaken using a curved steel bar to deflect and pre-tension a sheet of fabric stretched across a rectangular opening in a plywood sheet (Figure 8).

The bar was left exposed on the soffit; however this may be inappropriate in some practical applications. A series of prototype beams was constructed to investigate different methods of construction. A typical beam is essentially a T section in which the web tapers from a maximum depth and breadth at the mid-span to zero at the supports.

The overall length of the prototype beam is 3.16 m. The length of the web is 3 m, leaving an 80 mm projection of the flange at each end. The projection of the flange provides an effective bearing detail for the beam. A casting

rig was specially designed and constructed using two steel beams supporting an 18 mm thick plywood sheet. A rectangular piece of fabric was folded in two. The curved geometry of the web was determined by holding the folded fabric vertically and stretching a weighted cable between two points 3 m apart; the curve of the cable describes a parabola, the shape of the bending moment diagram for a uniformly distributed load. The sag of the cable was adjusted to give the required overall depth at the mid-span of the beam. The two sides of the fabric were stitched along this curve. An elongated elliptical hole was cut along the central axis of the plywood defining the intersection between the flange and the web (Figures 9 and 10).

The plywood was cut into two parts along the central axis of the elliptical hole to facilitate stripping of the formwork. The horizontal curve of the ellipse was obtained in the same way as the web. The fabric was then placed through the hole in the plywood in such a way that the two ends of the stitched curve coincided with the two points of the ellipse. The surplus material was attached, using staples, to the upper face of the plywood sheet. Weights were placed in the pocket formed by the folded fabric below the stitching to pre-tension the fabric before casting. The same fabric as the earlier beam, tradename Lotrak 50R, was used.[4] Lotrak 50R is a polypropylene geotextile fabric, with excellent strength and tear resistance; it is readily stitched using a domestic sewing machine and strips easily from the hardened concrete. The fabric costs approximately 0.5 euros per square metre. The beam was reinforced using two 10 mm mild steel bars, curved to follow the primary curve of the web. At the ends of the beam the reinforcement becomes horizontal and is anchored into the flange. The flange was reinforced with a 50 by 50 mm mesh with 3 mm diameter bars, positioned at the mid-depth of the flange.

In subsequent beams the construction process was developed to improve repeatability and consistency of casts and increase the control of the pre-tension. It was felt that the stitching of the curve relied on the skill of the students and that this could lead to inconsistencies between casts. The stitching was replaced by a pair of plywood curves that defined the profile of the web. The plywood curves were used to clamp the folded fabric sheets together. The ends of the plywood curves were attached to the underside of the plywood used to form the flange of the beam. Pre-tension was added to the formwork by stretching the fabric against the plywood curve. A series of beams was constructed. A careful survey of the cross section dimensions was carried out and they were found to be very consistent across the range of beams cast. The beams were also tested structurally until failure. As expected the beams tended to fail at the support, where the flange meets the web. Successive prototypes showed that the strength at the supports could be improved by altering the reinforcement pattern and the inclination of the reinforcement at the support. More significant however was a further modification that suggested itself by the process of construction. By simply curving the plywood sheet that supports the flange

upwards at mid-span it is possible to vary the thickness of the flange to give increased thickness at the supports. Structural testing of this arrangement was very successful, with greater strength than the previous beams but more significantly a change in failure mode. Failure occurred at the mid-span of the beam rather than the supports (see also Chapter 6). From a structural engineering perspective this is most satisfactory, as bending failure defines the upper limit of strength for a beam. Thus the geometry of the beam was optimised for structural performance, by placing the concrete exactly where needed. The beam is deep at mid-span and the flange is thicker at the supports where anchorage of the reinforcement is critical. The development of the beam demonstrates how the apparent complexity of the form provides a truly rational structure (Figure 11). The route to this result is through the construction process, iteration and reflection.

Columns

Columns are interesting structural and architectural forms. In terms of process, columns provide an opportunity to study how fabric can be used to create curved linear elements with a high ratio of fabric surface to total surface. Production involves casting vertically; therefore the height of the wet concrete creates high hydrostatic pressures at the base. It is essential to develop large tensions in the fabric to control bulging at the base. A specially designed, adaptable casting rig was designed for the columns. The rig consists of two horizontal steel frames covered with plywood. The frames are connected to vertical steel legs using adjustable brackets. The frames form the top and bottom surfaces of the column. A tube of fabric is passed through a hole in the lower frame and fixed to the underside of the plywood. A second sheet of plywood is attached to the underside of the first sheet, sealing the base of the column. The fabric tube is then fed through a similar hole in the upper frame and fixed to the topside of the plywood. This initial stretching takes most of the slackness out of the fabric. Further tension is induced in the fabric by jacking the

4
Geotextile fabrics are used in many below ground applications such as road construction, earth retaining structures and erosion control. Lotrak is manufactured and supplied by Don and Low Ltd, Forfar, Scotland.

9

10

11

Fig 9
Formwork for beam (R. Pedreschi)

Fig 10
Concrete beam (R. Pedreschi)

Fig 11
Final version of beam (D. Lee)

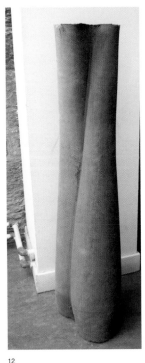

12

13a

13b

Fig 12
Initial prototype column
(R. Pedreschi)

Fig 13
Fabric formed columns
(R. Pedreschi)

top frame upwards using threaded steel rods. Concrete is then poured into the form through the top hole. The first experiment with this technique produced a rather sublime result. The plywood sheets were cut with an opening forming a figure of eight (Figure 12).

The cross section at the top and bottom of the column are prescribed by these forms; however the nature of the fabric and its response to the pressure of the wet concrete tend to push the fabric and hence the form of the column towards a circular cross section in the middle.

To maintain the cross sections geometry two thin steel strips were incorporated into the fabric and connected to the upper and lower plywood sheet. The strips were connected at the waist of the figures of eight, at the intersection of the two circles. The seams in the fabric were made by simply wrapping the edges of the fabric around the steel strip. The fabric was installed in the rig and tensioned. The top plywood sheet was rotated through 90°, adding further tension in the fabric. The tension in the fabric can be read in the smooth twisting curve of the column, accentuated by the control of the cross section geometry provided by the steel strap. The form tapers slightly from its base, further suggesting tension as the column appears to be twisted

upwards. This particular piece has stimulated a number of other ideas.

The use of fabric tubes, stretched and twisted, was studied in the development of a process to produce columns with voids. The fabric is folded over and stitched along one edge to create a tube. The tube is laid flat and the two sides stitched together with a round or rectangular pattern in the centre. The tube is then stretched and twisted and the concrete is poured. The stitched seam displaces the concrete to create voids in the finished element. The resulting form creates a column that splits from the base into two separate twisted columns that are then reunited at the head of the column (Figure 13).

The separation of the column creates a form that accentuates slenderness and twist to create an element of organic complexity. The technique to produce this form developed rapidly and a number of columns with varying fabrics, forms and details were made. An intriguing aspect was the development of the connection between the elements. As an individual piece each column can develop a form in response to its particular characteristics such as fabric, void and tension; however when the column is seen as an architectural component it becomes necessary to return to the matter

14a

14b

of connections. The aim was to develop connection details, raising the question of geometric precision. The approach to the problem may be defined by identifying and separating the general and the particular.

The general is consistent across all elements and forms the connection between. In this project an interlocking male and female connection was developed that would be dimensionally consistent for each element. The ends of each column were built to have corresponding interlocking ends. The geometric accuracy was ensured by developing a plastic moulding that was incorporated into the ends of the formwork. A wooden template was made for each of the male and female ends and the inserts formed by vacuum forming. The details were developed in a series of prototype connections (Figure 14). The prototype connections are independent of the columns and could be incorporated into other components. The section of the column between the connections is particular, depending on fabric, patterning and pre-tension. Thus geometric consistency between the ends of the columns was achieved. A series of columns was made which could be connected to each other in any sequence. The twist between the top and bottom could now be measured accurately using the precise geometry of the ends as a

datum. There is continuity of the twist across the three sections.

The technique for the incorporation of voids was developed further. In the previous example the construction process limited the column to two legs. Two legs may imply instability whilst three legs suggest stability. A different process was developed to create three legged columns that resulted in a different way of thinking about the process. Stitching was eliminated. Drawing reference from the beams plywood clamps were developed and used both to form the seams along the edge of the fabric and to displace the concrete to create voids. Three sheets of fabric were used and connected along their edges using plywood clamps bolted together (Figure 15).

The resulting columns were very different from the earlier ones. The surfaces became more complex and intricate, whilst the process was simplified. The formwork can be seen as a kit of parts to be assembled in a variety of ways, which again expresses the general and the particular. There is a wonderful interactivity with the construction process that allows the specific geometry of the surface to be determined during the assembly of the formwork. It is analogous to jazz music: the end conditions and the edge clamps create

15

Fig 14
Prototype column connection (R. Pedreschi)

Fig 15
Column formwork using plywood clamps (R. Pedreschi)

16

17

Fig 16
Fabric formed columns
(R. Pedreschi)

Fig 17
Hollow column
(R. Pedreschi)

Fig 18
Details of wall panels
(R. Pedreschi)

the overall form or the rhythm and melody of the composition, whilst the arrangements of voids and clamps are improvised solos. Like all good musicians the builder can develop his technique through practice (Figure 16).

Another project studied hollow columns, effectively concrete tubes with varying cross sections. Hollow concrete columns are not often used as it is difficult to provide the inner formwork unless the column is sufficiently large to allow access to remove it. In considering the expression of the surface and form one of the aims of a hollow column must be to present its inner surface; therefore the column should be pierced. Technically this is a complex problem. An inside and an outside fabric surface have to be created. The concrete then has to be poured in between the two while maintaining the tension on the fabric (Figure 17).

Punctures are formed in the wall of the column by stitching the two layers of fabric together. Through a series of prototypes the construction techniques were developed. Initial prototypes were unsuccessful as the inner fabric tended to collapse inwards. Eventually an effective construction process was developed. A plastic pipe was placed in the core and dry sand was packed between the column and inner fabric to provide support. A similar connection detail to that used in the previous columns was developed. Different fabrics were used for the inner and outer surfaces. The outer fabric used simple cotton material and the inner used a polyester with a regular grid of plastic squares bonded to it. The distorted fabric grid created a particularly interesting and unusual surface.

Walls

The dialogue between process and form follows another route when considering wall panels. Where it is desired to make a panel with two finished surfaces, as opposed to one, then a different process is required, conditioned by the need to develop tension in the fabric whilst controlling the geometry of two surfaces. Two separate processes were investigated, initiated by reflecting on two quite different potential applications. The first of these considered the wall as a perforated screen, made by a series of pre-cast panels. Timber side shutters were used to define the end of the panel, where one would butt against the other, controlling the geometry precisely where needed. It was also envisaged that the panels would sit on the edge of a floor slab and could be applied in a multi-storey building. How could these panels stack? What would be the detail at the slab edge? Again the fabric itself offered the solution. Adjusting the tension in the fabric at the base of the formwork allowed it to flow over the edge of a timber section, representing the slab. The upper part of the panel was designed to interlock with the succeeding panel above. The same formwork was used to cast three prototype panels at half scale. The panels were then assembled into a complete construction (Figure 18).

The second project was a study to test the application directly on a live architectural project, described in more detail in Chapter 3. The panel is intended as a privacy screen between the front doors of terraced housing whilst supporting a canopy overhead. In comparison with the preceding project the

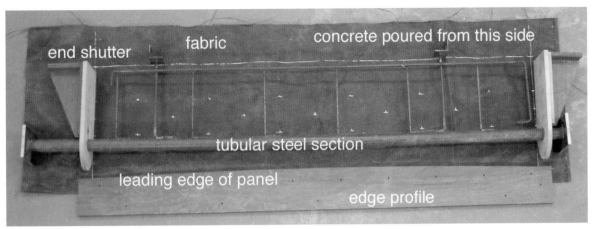

19

20

requirements were quite different, and these informed the casting technique used. The first things to consider are the critical surface edges. These are the two sides and the leading edge. The back edge and the top and bottom of the panels are not seen. The concrete panel is intended to float, touching neither the ground nor the canopy directly. A 50 mm diameter circular hollow section runs through the panel from the foundation to the underside of the canopy. The precise

dimensions of the cross section were conditioned by the steel section to ensure sufficient concrete around the section. The panel was cast using the same technique as the beam, with the leading edge of the panel formed by the plywood profile suspended at the bottom of the fabric (Figure 19).

Timber profiles with a slight curve were attached to two end panels which also held the steel section in position. The development of the formwork is illustrated in (Figure 20).

Fig 19
Components for production of the wall panels (R. Pedreschi)

Fig 20
Construction sequence for panel (R. Pedreschi)

21

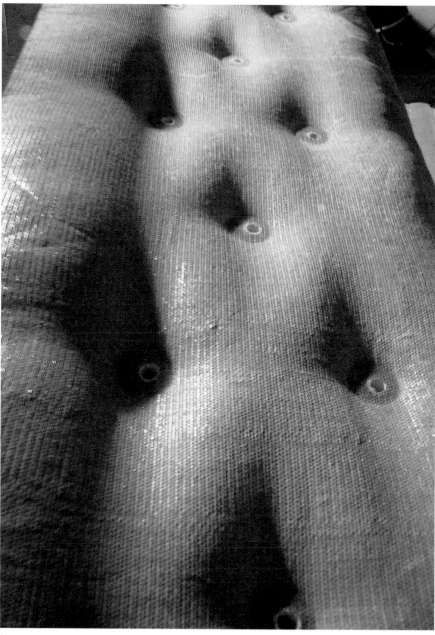

22

In the case of the beam the fabric was pulled
tightly against the timber profile to form a
sharp edge. In the panels the tension in the
fabric was reduced to form a rounded bull-
nose edge. The fabric was stripped from the
panels in the vertical position (Figure 21). The
geotextile fabric provided sheen to the panel
surface (Figure 22).

**Reflections on the
outcome of the studies**

To date the research programme has
completed 12 separate projects. Not all are

reported here. Collectively they provide a
broad perspective of the potential of fabric
formwork. The approach has been largely
one of 'enthusiastic scepticism': enthusiasm
about the idea but concern to establish a
realistic evaluation of the technology. In the
five-week–long student projects there was a
rapid growth in skills and confidence in both
design and construction that led to a series of
innovative constructions. Rather than limiting
the technology each project has revealed
further directions for study. The methodology,
focussing on process through sequential
prototyping, tends to edit out inappropriate

Fig 21
Stripping the fabric
(R. Pedreschi)

Fig 22
Wall panel surface
(R. Pedreschi)

technical solutions. Consequently there has been a progressive simplification of form and process of the existing typologies. The journey has been one of exploration, evaluation and development, essentially cyclical and iterative in nature. Take for example the beam. The first prototype demonstrated form, but raised questions regarding connection and the placing of the reinforcement. Subsequent prototypes found answers to these questions and the strength of the end anchorage improved through refinement of the reinforcement details. The third series of prototypes finally resolved the anchorage using geometry rather than steel to create a variable thickness flange. In comparison with planar, orthogonal formwork the multiple curves of the beam may appear complex; however when seen in terms of the use of fabric as formwork, it is the result of a rational and logical development of form, process and detail.

The dichotomy in classification between form and process remains. Consideration of form is useful in relation to description of the finished object. Process represents a series of sequential activities directed towards a particular aim. The complexity of process is closely related to the complexity of surface. A simple measure of surface complexity relates the ratio of fabric surface to total surface in the finished object. In all casts there will be surfaces that are not conditioned by the fabric, formed by either the hole on the top of the formwork through which the concrete is poured or the surface created by the incorporation of non-fabric elements included to control geometry at specific points in the object. The table below identifies these characteristics. As the ratio of exposed fabric to total surface increases, the research has shown a corresponding increase in the intricacy of the construction process, both in the formwork itself and in the control of the tension in the fabric.

This becomes self evident when comparing the ease of casting a simple panel, where the proportion of fabric surface area to total area is approximately 50 per cent, with the hollow column, where the proportion is around 95 per cent. The table demonstrates the importance of process as a method of informing design. Comparing the two wall panels helps to illustrate this point. Although both walls required fabric surfaces on both sides, the second panel was cast using the same techniques as the beam. For this reason the construction was simpler as the formwork was more accessible, the concrete had less distance to travel and there was also greater control over the critical leading edge.

The role of the builder or maker of fabric cast concrete involves both the deconstruction of the object into a sequence of steps and the continual re-evaluation and adjustment of the form during the assembly and casting process. The design develops during the making. It is analogous to rubble walling. The overall size, the height and length of the wall are predetermined but the actual arrangement of stones is only finalised during construction.

In conclusion, the power of the underlying idea of fabric formwork is best understood by returning to the discussion about viewing position. There have been many visitors to the Architecture workshop, including architects, engineers, builders, pre-cast concrete producers and fabric technologists, who provide these multiple points of view. They seemed to share an instinctive reaction that warms to the combination of the pragmatic, the expressive and the rational spirit – a combination of craft and technology often missing in many contemporary construction processes. Perhaps it is the traces of humanity rather than the machine that is evident are the constructions, a consequence of the dialogue between process and form.

RATIO OF FABRIC SURFACE TO TOTAL SURFACE	CHARACTERISTICS	TYPES OF ELEMENT	ORIENTATION	COMPLEXITY OF PROCESS
Low	Horizontal, planar elements	Panels	Inverted	Low
Medium	Linear, horizontally cast	Beams	Finished	Medium
High	Linear, vertically cast	Columns and walls	Finished	High
Very high	Linear, vertically cast	Hollow columns	Finished	Very high

form follows fabric

Fiona McLachlan

1
Such as their
archery range at
Barcelona 1989–91
(El Croquis 49/50,
pp.32–69). Similar
mathematically
generated curves
are found in the
work of Eladio Dieste
and Heinz Isler.

2
Rudolf Steiner
Goetheanum at
Dornach near
Basel, Switzerland
1925–28.

Introduction

Casting concrete in fabric creates an inherent paradox. The relationship of materiality and form seems contradictory, in that something so inherently strong and utilitarian, with its associations of Minimalism and Brutalism, can be so flowing, soft and textured. That concrete is a fluid when cast, and its form is utterly dependent on the mould in which it is cast, means that it is capable of taking any form, and yet the predominant forms it is seen to take in the built environment are rectilinear. Enormous efforts are made on the part of the industry to ensure that formwork is straight, tightly constructed and will not deform when the concrete is being poured.

Over the last few years, as experiments with the process have been under way at Edinburgh University, pieces of concrete have gradually appeared around the architecture school (Figure 1). Most architects visiting the school seem to have the same reaction. To look is not enough – the pieces seem to demand touch.

Photographs of I.M. Pei's National Gallery East Wing in Washington DC. (1978) tell a similar story. The acute angle of sharp white stone is marked by the dullness of thousands of hand prints. Rarely does architecture have this effect, being most associated with the visual,

or perhaps the haptic sense of experiencing space. With fabric cast concrete, the material is tactile, perhaps most particularly because of the curving forms, and the variety of surface finishes that are so readily made by the process.

Most architects and students of architecture will be aware how difficult it is to perfect curved lines, with many attempts producing clumsy results. The most successful seem to be those that are mathematically generated, such as the early work of Enric Miralles and Carmé Pinos.[1] The more accurately the curve is defined by geometry – tangents, lines and arcs – the more satisfying the result. Flowing forms have suffered further compromise in concrete construction. The curving planes at Rudolf Steiner's second Goetheanum at Basel are crude interpretations of his 1:100 model.[2] The formwork required for this exceptional building had to perform complex gymnastics using timber boards and cages of reinforcement. The final forms, while expressive of the process, are somewhat compromised by the need to accommodate facets of the timber boards rather than being able to follow 'pure' curves. There are other established methods, such as the use of sprayed concrete on mesh. This was

1

Fig 1
Test column by students
C. Khoo, W. Wang and
others

3

*Professor Mark West,
Director of the Centre for
Architectural Structures
and Technology (CAST)
University of Manitoba,
Canada.*

4

Author of The art of
precast concrete, *2005
and other notable books
on concrete.*

5

*In an email from Hugh
Strange, project architect,
January 2007.*

2

3

Fig 2
Laced concrete column

Fig 3
The Collection, Lincoln

notably used by Günther Domenig in his
Zentralsparkasse bank in Vienna (1979) and
relies on a complex matrix of mesh to define
the form, the concrete being applied as a
surface skin.

As Mark West noted on his first visit to
Edinburgh in 2004, with fabric cast concrete,
you pour the concrete 'and God makes the
form'.[3] The forces of nature, gravity and the
inherent properties of the material will define
beams which directly correspond to their
bending moments, providing more concrete
where stresses are highest. Of course, it is
not quite as easy as that. Our experiments
have concluded that the more precision in the
setting out of the fabric, the better the result.
There are analogies with dressmaking, with
early attempts being stitched on a sewing
machine – an incongruous piece of equipment
in a workshop. One was threaded together
like a bodice, the fabric being pulled together
with laces (Figure 2). As with the work of
fashion designers, the cut is all-important if a
predictable result is to be achieved.

This chapter will reflect on the design and
manufacture of two experimental fabric cast
panels for a social housing project in central
Scotland, discussions with an industrial
partner, and the development of the technique
using steel imprints to form traced patterns on
the surface of the concrete.

Predictability is core to the process of
architecture. Architects and engineers
need to be able to give a requisite level of
certainty to the client, and few projects could
accommodate a 'wait and see' attitude to
concrete design. The need for predictability
in structural design is also an imperative, and
structural engineers will need greater certainty
in the performance of the material to feel
comfortable in designing structural elements
using the technique. Yet part of the inherent
appeal of insitu concrete is its unpredictability
– the key issue is the ability to control this to
within acceptable limits.

David Bennett,[4] in a lecture at Edinburgh
University, gave the students a 'recipe'
for concrete. 'Understand and adhere to
this advice and you won't go wrong,' he
assured them. The analogy with cooking
was clear, the ingredients being simple but
with the possibility of failure if the mix is
wrong, the formwork is poorly constructed
or the conditions are not carefully monitored.
Whereas in much cooking some leeway is
tolerable, casting concrete is like baking
bread: it needs precision to be predictable and
repeatable.

One key aspect of concrete is that no two
casts will be exactly alike – the shade,
the position of the minute air bubbles, the

mix, water content and temperature of the
environment are all factors that can affect
the outcome. Specification of insitu concrete
is critical, and Bennett clearly believes
knowledge and understanding of the mix to
be a key tool for an architect who wishes to
exploit the qualities of exposed concrete.
Knowledge continues to develop along with
new processes. The creamy striped limestone
exterior walls at The Collection, Lincoln by
Panter Hudspith, are complemented by
interior walls of 'self-compacting concrete'
(Figure 3). This is an expensive material, which
is poured in layers, allowing a slight bulge
in the stripes, which catches the light and is
very appropriate to the museum's collection
of historical and archaeological artifacts.
The architects have noted [5] that the qualities
they wanted to achieve were those of mass,
solidity, permanence and history, alluding to
the work of Svere Fehn and Peter Zumthor at
Vals (although admittedly in stone).

The unpredictability of the final result appealed
to the architects, but also demanded a
leap of a faith from the client. The technical
properties of the material, as well as its visual
possibilities, were essential in making a case
for its use, providing the environmental stability
essential to the building, which is a container
of valuable archaeological objects.

This use of a new variant of concrete has
parallels with the development of fabric cast
concrete and, in particular, its transferability
to the building industry. At the time of going
to tender for the Lincoln project, the ability to
try to control the construction quality through
clauses within the specification were limited
to an architects' addendum to the structural
engineers' specification referring to the finish
quality. It takes the designer, contractor and
client collectively to take such an element of
risk prior to a standardization of specification
and the process of normalization that occurs
as shared knowledge develops. In some
respects, self-compacting concrete, as
Bennett notes, 'is just too plastic – as there
are no blow holes it just doesn't look like
concrete, more like ceramic'.[6]

As with any new constructional technique, the
initial research and development demands
a disproportionate investment of time and
allowance for trial and error. As noted by
Hugh Strange,[7] accommodating such
experimentation within a normal building
contract is demanding: 'At the end of the day
though, however much you do, you can't
completely control the results, and that's part
of the enjoyment – the variation.'

Indeed Adrian Forty has argued that it is a
mistake to designate concrete as a material:
'Concrete, let us be clear, is not a material, it
is a process' (2006, p.35). Indeterminacy is its

very nature. The limitations and possibilities are dependent on interpretation by architect and contractor.

It has been suggested that concrete shares some essential characteristics with stone. It can be cut, tooled and shaped (see Heinle and Bacher 1971, p.65), but with concrete the casting process creates form and material simultaneously rather than consecutively. The scope for uncertainty in the process, and the resultant material, are part of the creative and intellectual challenge of designing with concrete.

Formwork

The open ended interpretation of concrete has at times resulted in ambiguity, either through trying to emulate stone, or to obscure the process by post-casting treatments of the surface. Its most natural expression, as product of a process, is part of its appeal.

The re-emergence of board-marked concrete in the Walsall Art Gallery by Caruso St John (2000), and in the central internal void at Dance City, Newcastle upon Tyne, by Malcolm Fraser Architects (2006), suggests that architects continue to enjoy the roughness of concrete and the ability to express traces of the process of making in concrete. Clive Albert, project architect of Dance City, noted that they had to 'relax the tolerance' on the shuttering to achieve an acceptably uneven character for the concrete.[8] The irregularity of the concrete was designed as a counterpoint to the very precise brickwork on the exterior of the building. The boards were fixed to a backing of plywood and then set in position prior to the pouring of the concrete, and the board lining was permitted to deviate by a maximum of 7 mm between butting boards, with the concrete being allowed to

ooze slightly (see Figures 4,5). At Lincoln, the formwork was similar, using horizontal boards planed to varying thicknesses and randomly placed, but unlike a traditional mix, self-consolidating concrete does not require the use of vibrators to achieve an even fill of the formwork. The surface quality is therefore more predictable, but there remains a degree of randomness in the result.

This desire for a degree of imperfection and unpredictability is a common reason for using board-marked concrete, but the imperfection is defined by highly controlled limits. Cracks, which produce leakages, or unintended bulges due to deformed shutters, are less appealing. Inviting deliberate deformation of the mould itself, as is seen in the fabric cast process, requires a completely different attitude to the process.

Surface

Early experiments in fabric cast concrete by Honours students at Edinburgh University in 2004, with Professors Mark West and Remo Pedreschi, demonstrated the potential of the process. It was immediately clear that the more precise the fabric form, the better the results. As an understanding of the consequences of the method developed, it became easier to predict the likely deformations that would occur. 'Stretchy' fabric yields bulbous forms but is more difficult to control. The finest detail of the fabric is imprinted into the concrete, and because the fines naturally come to the surface owing to the permeable formwork, the concrete has a surface of great strength.

The use of geotextile membrane seemed to offer the best results as being a strong, flexible but dimensionally stable material. It leaves a fine chequered pattern and a slight sheen on the surface, which is likely to fade gradually.

6

Quoted from a lecture at Edinburgh University November 2006.

7

Hugh Strange is a graduate of Edinburgh University and was Panter Hudspith's project architect for the Collection at Lincoln completed in 2005, which won The Concrete Building of the Year 2006 and was nominated for the prestigious Gulbenkian Award in 2006. Self-compacting concrete was also used at the Phaeno Science Center at Wolfsburg (2005) by Zaha Hadid Architects.

8

From a conversation with Clive Albert 3 January 2007. Dance City was completed in October 2005; the client was Dance City/Newcastle City Council and the contractor was Shepherd Construction

Fig 4
Stair under construction, Dance City, Newcastle, Malcolm Fraser Architects

Fig 5
Central space complete, Dance City, Newcastle, Malcolm Fraser Architects

9
The author is a partner
in E & F McLachlan
Architects with Ewen
McLachlan.

7

6

8, 9

Fig 6
Experimental panel cast
horizontally, and then
inverted, University of
Edinburgh (2004)

Fig 7
Housing at Whitburn,
West Lothian –
site layout model

Fig 8, 9
Housing at Whitburn,
West Lothian –
early computer models

Smoother surfaces can be made in cotton, but with the disadvantage that it is more difficult to strip the cast. Geotextile is relatively cheap, and while the best results were with a new sheet of material, it can be cleaned, and if stripped carefully can be re-used, which would be important should the process be transferred to industrial production.

The tendency of the concrete to form the most natural economical shape is discussed in other chapters.

Precast panels were an obvious starting point as, being non-structural, there were no issues with the lack of test data on the material. Early experiments (Figure 6) demonstrated how sensitive the appearance was to lapses in time between one bucket of concrete and the next, with 'tide marks' or pockmarks being created in the surface.

The first opportunity to use fabric cast concrete on a 'live' project came in a social housing project at Whitburn in West Lothian,

by the practice E & F McLachlan Architects for Horizon Housing Association. The layout for the development utilizes housing in straight lines set parallel to the roadway, designed to relate to the existing linear urban form of the town (Figure 7). The clean lines of the housing contrast with the natural forms of the adjacent woodland and naturalized swales being constructed on site.

One of the interests of the practice has been the development of a common language for a series of housing projects in urban, suburban and rural sites: the manipulation of external space to form external rooms; the implicit control of public and private areas through the forms of the buildings and their relationships; the use of simple, robust and economical materials. At Whitburn, emphasis was given to the grouping of entrance doors in either pairs or fours to encourage chance meetings between neighbours (Figure 8). The expression of the entrance doors as key architectural elements was developed from the client's brief.

Early computer models showed a simple rectangular concrete fin between the paired house entrances with a steel column supporting a canopy over (Figure 9). As the project developed, the opportunity to make fins using fabric cast concrete was explored.

Developing the panels

One of the key differences between early workshop experiments and this real situation was the precision required to work within actual built dimensions and within a contractual programme.[10]

Sterling Precast were the supplier being used by the main contractor on the project for the supply of precast sills and window surrounds (Figure 10). Their normal method of manufacture is to dry cast using moulds made in their workshop. They also make some wet cast components, but have found that the dry cast method is fastest for the production of these particular elements, allowing an early stripping of the moulds. It has the disadvantage of being more easily chipped on site or during handling, but can achieve sharp profiles.

Representatives from Sterling Precast visited the workshop early in the project in order to ascertain wether they would be willing to participate in the trial manufacture of the panels.[11] It was useful to discuss the technique with a manufacturer, and show them the display of student work. A prototype panel was then made.

The first prototype was made fullsize using some of the techniques learnt from the early studies (Figure 11). The panel used circular tubes drawn together on threaded screws to tighten the fabric in a regular pattern.

Professor Remo Pedreschi calculated the fabric pattern to allow for a gently curving profile to the vertical front edge of the panel, and sufficient excess fabric to give a rounded, softly bulging appearance between the restrained points.

The method adopted was to cast it as a vertical pour, but set on its long edge, so that the ends were restrained by plywood shutters cut to a curving profile. The fabric hung as a sling between the supporting top edges. The lowest edge was clamped between pieces of plywood to ensure that the line was controlled. Once cast and stripped, the panel was rotated to the vertical.

This prototype allowed us to confirm that the method of casting, reinforcement, steel column and overall profile of the end pieces were satisfactory.

Further discussions took place with Sterling as industrial partner, and the project's structural engineer. These were very positive, and a method was agreed by which the work could be shared between the University and the precast manufacturer.

Although the first panel pattern was successful, it was felt that the design could be made to have more meaning to the particular project. A new technique was developed to use steel patterns to cast an imprint into the surface of the fabric. Square-section steel rods were bent and clamped either side of the fabric in a simple S-shaped curve with threaded rods joining the steel front and back (Figure 12). The square section formed a defined width of imprint in the cast surface. Any pattern could be used, and did not need to be the same on both sides. It is also possible to make holes by pulling the fabric tightly together so that the concrete does not fill the void.

10

The project had its own structural engineer, The Structural Partnership (Glasgow), the main contractor was J.B. Bennetts and the precast concrete supplier was Sterling Precast.

11

At this point in time, five panels were required.

11

Fig 10
Precast window surrounds on site at Whitburn

Fig 11, 12
Prototype panels, University of Edinburgh

10   12

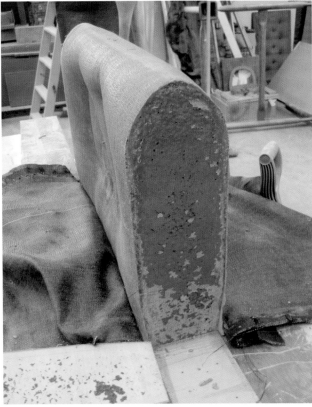

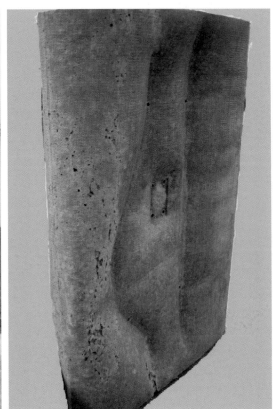

13

15

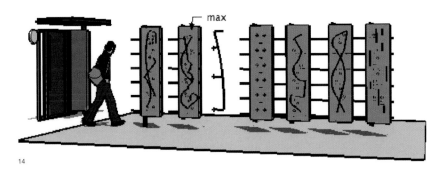

14

The test demonstrated that if the fabric is too restrained by closely spaced rods the curves are lost and the profile becomes flat. The optimum is to achieve some bulging of the fabric in order to bring out the qualities of the process in making curving forms that would be impossible in conventional shuttering (Figure 13). When it becomes flattened, the pattern is less distinct.

The design was developed through a series of studies of lines and curves (Figure 14). The final design was based on an abstracted map of the town of Whitburn.

A third trial panel was cast using a test part plan taken from the map with rectangles of steel either side, used to signify the site

(Figure 15). By pulling this slightly closer together than the rest of the steel pattern, the site became more deeply imprinted. Some parts of the steel pattern that came close to a vertical edge were canted slightly to maintain the straight line of the rear edge profile. Any section that came close to the curving front edge made a slightly clumsy indent in the profile, which would need to be avoided.

The final pattern was adjusted to take account of the results of the test panels, and drawn fullsize onto a template so that the steelwork could be formed by hand matching the template. A mirror image of the steelwork was formed and the two joined by threaded screws.

16   17   18

Prototype to production

The interest shown by Sterling Precast was encouraging, and allowed discussion to take place on the issues generated by exporting the process from prototype to a commercial production.

Sterling Precast were interested in the project as part of their continuing research and development programme. In common with many long-established but relatively small businesses, they rarely have any time to undertake research, especially during periods of high demand. The rising cost of timber is a key issue, as the majority of their moulds are timber, which although re-usable many times eventually wear out. For their mainstream activity of producing high quality dry cast elements for the house building industry, the fabric cast process has little to offer at present. The speed of production of dry cast products, despite their highly handcrafted nature, allows two men to produce up to 40 sills in a day. This re-constituted 'stone' is most appropriate for elements with flat, angular surfaces, almost the antithesis of the fabric cast process. The moulds are struck almost immediately after being filled, and are then float finished by hand (Figures 16, 17).

The fabric cast technique may be more transferable to bespoke wet cast products, which Sterling also make, and which commonly take a full day to cure. The robustness of the fabric cast surface had an immediate appeal, and the lack of problems with hydration staining would reduce wastage. All of Sterling's products require a flat bench surface to support the moulds, whereas the fabric process can be suspended rather than propped, giving direct access to the base of the mould. This could be attractive in the making of arches and beams, which are presently cast on the flat.

Economic realities predominate and it is not, at present, obvious how this particular manufacturer could adopt the fabric cast process, but they are aware that circumstances change in the industry and that the high demand for cast 'stone' may decline, as it did in the 1970s and early 1980s, when facing brick was more universally used. Rather than trying to replicate the existing dry cast products, the fabric cast technique offers an opportunity for the development of a new range of components, making use of the ease of achieving curved profiles for a market yet to be defined.

For various reasons, the number of panels required in the Whitburn project reduced from five to two and, at this point, it was clear that it would be easier for the University to cast the panels. Sterling Precast would have had to break off from their production to make a cradle and to learn a new technique at a point when their plant was overstretched. Most small companies are so engrossed in the day-to-day running of the business that they are not able to develop new processes and products. For Sterling Precast, dry casting remains the most appropriate method for their core business. There was also a concern at the University that transferring the technique to a factory-based production might reduce the quality of the panels because of the care required in cutting the fabric, tailoring it around the end restraints, and the subtle differences produced as the tension of the fabric is modified to develop the required shape.

The structural design of the canopy was modified in discussion with the consultant engineer because of the difficulty of achieving a sufficient support from the brickwork skin and accommodating movement in the timber frame, and secondary thin, tubular supports were added at either end. These were

Fig 16, 17
Dry cast sills being manufactured at Sterling Precast, Stirling

Fig 18
Concrete fin at doorways, McMartin Court, Whitburn, May 2007

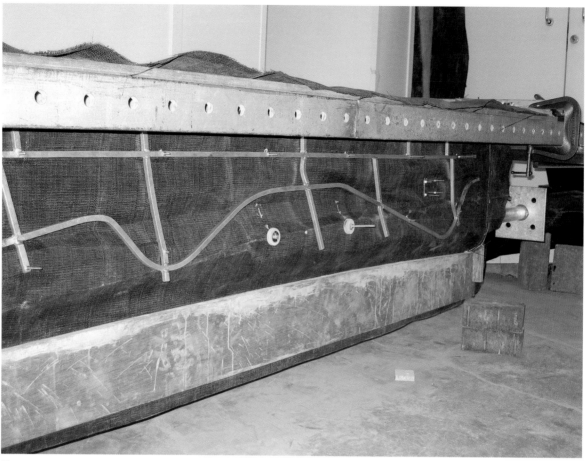

19

Figures 19, 20
Final panel manufacture
in the workshop

designed to act as gateposts to the mild steel railings and garden gates.

The making of the two final panels confirmed that it would have been difficult to communicate the sensitivity of the construction process to an industrial partner. Although detailed drawings were made, the fabric formwork was adjusted a number of times prior to the concrete being poured (Figure 19). Small plastic tube spacers were used to sheath the threaded tie rods to set the minimum distance at the key points along the steel pattern, and these were re-cut to adjust the amount of concrete cover to the main steel support pole. This is set into the concrete and extends beyond the panel to fix up to the canopy overhead. Additional adjustment was made to the tension in the fabric, and to the position of the tie rods to give additional fabric in the central areas but, critically, to

prevent the fabric bulging over what would be the vertical front edge. The curving panel edge is at hand height, and one would expect visitors will use the panel to prop themselves as they chat, and to touch it. It was essential that the front edge was restrained in the sling to achieve a straight, vertical line, but to leave enough free fabric to form a smooth curve. All of these adjustments were predictions, examining the fabric and trying to visualize the effect once the concrete filled the fabric. It is difficult to see how this could be achieved without the use of prototypes (Figure 20) and the knowledge gained from the previous experiments. Of the time taken to cast the panel, approximately 90 per cent was in preparing the formwork, making adjustments to achieve a precise setting out for the panel in relation to the steel canopy to the houses, and using judgement based on an understanding of the process to modify the amount of free

20

fabric between restrained points to give the desired curving surfaces. The final panels demonstrated the high quality of surface texture and form that can be achieved.

The process of fabric casting for this project is more akin to a bespoke commission rather than the manufacture of standard components. Although the development of the beam has reached the stage of repeatability and consistency, for one-off installations, as with timber and stone, there will always be a reliance on the craft and technical skills of the makers. Unlike board-marked or indeed heavily tooled concrete, it does not seek to express what Reyner Banham called 'the traces of contingencies and accidents of human fallibility and of human hand' (1966, p.16). The best results are derived by precision and calculation. Knowledge, derived from observation, analysis and discovery of

the process, reduces the unpredictability and establishes fabric casting as a viable alternative to traditional methods of casting.

If, as Forty (2006, p.34) notes, some of the discomfort of concrete as a material is that it has no intrinsic aesthetic, but 'rather too many', fabric cast concrete offers yet another expression. There is clearly no such thing as an honest expression of concrete if, indeed, one accepts that it is merely a product of process, but concrete cast in fabric is closest to its expression as a liquid, frozen in flowing forms.

jigging with concrete

matter and form in the making of Wall One
Katie Lloyd Thomas

Introduction

*Either the Creator ... or else Prometheus ...
took the new-made earth which, only recently
separated from the lofty aether, still retained
some elements related to those of heaven
and, mixing it with rainwater, fashioned it into
the image of the all-governing gods. Whereas
other animals hang their heads and look at the
ground, he made man stand erect, bidding
him look up to heaven, and lift his head to the
stars. So the earth, which had been rough and
formless, was moulded into the shape of a
man, a creature till then unknown.*

Ovid, Metamorphoses, *p.31*

It bulges. It strains. The concrete mass of Wall
One shows all the signs of its liquid weight
pushing out against the restraints which kept
it upright while it was being formed. It retains
the imprints of the cable and ply disc corset
which prevented it from following concrete's
fluid nature, its sluggish certain tendency to
become horizontal. It reveals the complex
process which held it vertical and insisted it
became a wall not a floor. .

On the one hand, Wall One can be seen
as one of a family of constructions where
material is allowed to find its own form.

Gaudi's famous assemblage of suspended
chains 'found' the inverted structural form of
the Sagrada Famila (see Burry, 1999). Frei
Otto developed tensile membranes from the
'self-formations' of soap film surfaces (see
Otto and Rausch 1995). More recently Nox
has moved from digitally driven form-finding
to an interest in the material emergence of
form, for example through growing latex
lattices (see Spuybroek 2004). Form is not
imposed on to the material but seems to
come from within, and the specific properties
of each material affect the outcome. These
examples, however, generate a form which is
then translated with great difficulty into another
material at a different scale. A set of chains
hang easily as catenary arches but become a
constructional irrationality taking decades to
complete when cut into pieces of stone. Otto's
delicate soap film surfaces are recreated at
vast scale as fabric membranes or steel nets.
Both constructional and structural logic are
abandoned in the translation of Nox's lattices,
which are cut and assembled out of a series
of rigid two dimensional plywood pieces. What
marks fabric formwork out as a technique
is that no translation occurs. In the making
of Wall One the construction is both the
generation of the form, and the final form itself.

1

For accounts of history, philosophy and science in relation to emergence see particularly Manuel De Landa 1997 and 2002.

On the other hand, Wall One seems to be produced through an extremely controlled process of fabrication. Precise understanding of the details, mixes of concrete and properties of materials to be used in fabric formwork has been developed since the 1960s and informs the construction of Wall One. And in this particular case the overall form – a section of a wall which could be repeated to make a sine curve – was also complex and highly determined (interestingly this intention can best be seen in the snaking slot cut into the ply base – the plan is often the site where the conceptual is most visible). It was at the level of detail that the outcome was undetermined. The spacings of pegs and clamps could alter the number and degree of undulations. The thicknesses of the wall, surface, texture and colour could be varied according to the proportions and aggregates used in the mix. But if concrete is to resist gravity and become a wall at all its casting must also be controlled.

This tension must be at work to some extent in all forms of construction, but in Wall One it becomes particularly visible because the material's own forces are allowed to play a determining part in the generation of its outcome. The current fascination with emergent behaviour of all kinds is widespread, both as a physical explanation – the growth of coral and crystals, weather and economic events – and as a conceptual framework.[1] Its appeal to architects is many sided – from the complexity of the forms which are arrived at to the quest for structural or 'natural' (if not constructional) efficiency or an interest in the concept of self generation. The focus here, however, will be the extent to which these techniques challenge the conventional relationship between form and matter in architecture.

Typically architects use parameters such as function or a set of ideas about proportion and symmetry to come to a formal design which is laid out in drawing to become a kind of virtual formwork for the building's material realization. Through these stages, the architect's formal vision is imposed on the material. In Wall One and the examples from Gaudi, Otto and Knox, architects choose instead to let the design emerge out of another parameter – material behaviour. Rather than shaping matter in a predetermined way the form arises, at least to some extent, out of the material. The form/matter model is not only the paradigm for most architectural discourse and practice, it also informs our world view and is the basis for most philosophical accounts of matter since Aristotle.

According to hylomorphism – as the form/matter model is often called in philosophical texts – form is active and imposes itself on matter which is inert, passive and merely receptive. Hylomorphism is a peculiarly static account in three ways. First, it does not encompass the possibility that matter might itself be active (or that it could generate form as in the above examples). Second, it describes form-taking in hierarchical terms where matter is dominated by form. And third – according to the French philosopher Gilbert Simondon in his extensive critique of hylomorphism (1964) – the schema assumes that individuality – what distinguishes one entity from another – can be found in the individual object rather than in the processes that give rise to it. This chapter shows how Wall One challenges each one of these three implications of the form/matter schema. In order to understand the hylomorphism at work in most architectural practice I use two very detailed specifications for concrete casting: one for a smooth modernist concrete wall and another for a brutalist concrete wall where the shuttering leaves its mark. How might Wall One challenge existing notions of form and matter, and does it suggest a more appropriate schema with which to describe the relationships involved in fabrication?

Forming concrete: material as matter in conventional casting

The concrete of Wall One is exceedingly delicate. As the water sweated out it brought the finest particles to the surface. They register the minute tracery of the geotextile weave and the indentations of cables and discs. Voids where water evaporated pockmark the surface; the crazings of a once living process. Two ragged openings scar the undulating form horizontally; ruptures where the three pours failed to meet smoothly. Here the concrete's own formations take over the subtle imprint of the textile, the change in colour above and below reveals the different mixes. Materials, moisture, internal and external forces, reactions and time are etched into the heavy mass (See Figure 1).

Conventional concrete casting exemplifies the shaping of inert matter by form. Concrete is a material with properties that make it a good model for the philosophical concept of matter. It is yielding, malleable and can be formed into any shape. It is, at least in its liquid state, without a particular form of its own. Aristotle chooses to use bronze in his account of matter (1988, p.174) and René Descartes selects wax (1968, pp.108–112). These materials are similar: they are formless in their

1

2
*For details of this
building see Gould
1977 and Architectural
Review 1935.*

molten state and can be melted down and
remade into any shape.

For Roland Barthes plastic is another
material with these matter-like qualities.
First, it seems to have no properties of its
own and instead mimics the properties of
other materials. Second, it is, he writes, 'the
very idea of its infinite transformation'. Third,
this transformation seems to take place
effortlessly, as if it is nothing more than a
seamless reshaping. He describes a machine
which churned out plastic objects and uses
the terms of hylomorphism. This production
demonstrates, he writes:

*the transmutation of matter. An ideally shaped
machine, tabulated and oblong (a shape well
suited to suggest the secret of an itinerary)
effortlessly draws, out of a heap of greenish
crystals, shiny and fluted dressing-room tidies.
At one end raw, telluric matter, at the other, the
finished, human object; and between these
two extremes, nothing; nothing but a transit.
(2000, p.97)*

Concrete, like plastic, exemplifies the concept
of matter but other materials would not
perform so well. Stone is not so 'yielding'.
Cloth cannot be melted down. Charcoal
cannot be infinitely transformed. These
materials all resist notions of transmutation
and it is no surprise that Aristotle and other
hylomorphic philosophers fail to mention them
in their accounts of matter.

Moreover, as a matter-like material concrete
lends itself well to a process of making which
is highly controlled and where the means of
fabrication and indeed the material's own
properties disappear from view. Traditional
rigid formwork and its related finishing
techniques might be understood rather like
Barthes' plastic moulding machine. They
aim to present the casting of concrete as if
it is produced in a seamless transit from raw
matter to finished object. For example in a
rather typical modernist house that Tecton
and Valentine Harding designed at Farnham
Common in 1934–35[2] the external concrete
walls were to be polished to a perfectly

3

There are two curved walls in the Harding house but they are constructed from blockwork – not concrete – and rendered with a thick plaster.

4

The school, in South London, was designed in 1961 and built in 1963/4. It was designed by John Bancroft at the LCC, who went on to design the better known Pimlico School. For more details see Bancroft 1973, pp.192–193.

2

3

94. The cement shall be stored in such a manner that it will be efficiently protected from moisture and the consignments can be used up in the order in which they are received.

95. No cement which has become damaged in the storage shall be used in the work, and all lumps must be removed.

AGGREGATE.   96. The aggregate shall be composed of hard stone or ballast, free from clay, dirt or other deleterious matter.   It shall pass through a ¾ inch screen and be thoroughly graded from coarse to fine.

97. The aggregate shall not be composed of flat or flaky materials.

98. Coal residues, such as coke breeze and clinkers, shall not be used for reinforced concrete work unless specifically approved in writing by the Architects or Engineers.

99. The aggregates to be used are presumed to be of a nature and quality necessary for the production of concrete which will give a crushing strength of not less than 3,000 lbs at the expiration of three months. When the concrete, made from such materials, is exposed to the weather or has to retain water, the materials shall be of such a nature that the concrete will resist the passage of water.   All concrete materials supplied shall be subject to the approval of the Architects or Engineers.

WATER.   100. The water shall be fresh water, clean and free from organic impurities.

PROPORTIONS.   101. That portion of the aggregate which is retained on a ¼ inch screen shall be termed "coarse aggregate" and that portion which passes a ¼ inch screen shall be termed "fine aggregate".

102. The 1 : 2½ : 5 concrete shall be composed of 1 part cement, 2½ parts sand and 5 parts coarse aggregate.

103. The 1 : 2 : 4 concrete shall be composed of 1 part cement, 2 parts sand and 4 parts coarse aggregate.

104. The materials shall be measured in vessels or containers of a nature which make reasonably accurate measurements possible.

105. The Contractor may, or shall if called upon, vary the proportion of fine to coarse aggregate with a view to obtaining the densest mix, provided the amount of cement per cubic yard of concrete in position is not reduced.

FORM WORK.   106. Form work must be erected true to line; be properly braced and of sufficient strength to carry the dead weight of the concrete with any constructional loads without excessive deflection.

13.

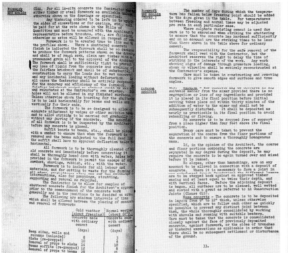
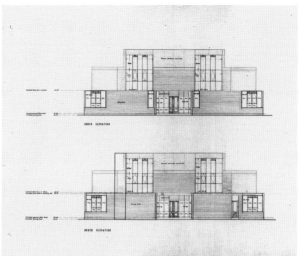

4   5

smooth surface after casting (Figures 2, 3). As
Harding stated in the Specification of Works:

EXTERNAL FINISH
111.
The shuttering for the external surfaces of all
walls, reveals, copings, soffits and fascias
must be perfectly smooth. As soon as the
shuttering is struck and while the concrete is
still green the above mentioned surfaces must
be rubbed down with a wood float and sand
till perfectly smooth. On no account must a
cement grout be used. (Harding 1934, p.14)

Here the finished concrete is intended to
appear as amorphous matter which can be
formed perfectly into the orthogonal shapes
described by the architect's modernist
concept.[3]

FORMWORK
106.
Formwork must be erected true to line; be
properly braced and of sufficient strength to
carry the dead weight of the concrete with
any constructional loads without excessive
deflection. (ibid., p.12)

Through a rigid formwork, form determines
matter which must submit to its orders. The
concrete matter must not affect the formwork
in any way or bring any inflection into the
encounter between the two.

In the Elfrida Rathbone School for the
Educationally Subnormal designed by John
Bancroft for the LCC in 1961 the marks of
the timber shuttering were to be left in the
exposed concrete walls to the raised assembly
hall (Figures 4, 5):

C14A FORMWORK AND MOULDS
Formwork is to be erected true to line and
to the profiles shown. Where a shuttered
concreted finish is indicated the formwork
shall be so designed to produce the formwork
patterns shown on the drawing and shall
be of rough sawn, clean new timber with a
pronounced grain all to the approval of the
Architect ... Boltholes will not be allowed in
any finished surfaces. (Bancroft 1961, p.31)[4]

Although one aspect of the fabrication
is registered in these concrete walls, the
architect edits others from the finished
product. He insists that the grain of the
shuttering is inscribed into the finished wall but
traces of the boltholes must disappear. He is
concerned also that the aggregate does not
interfere with the fine tracery of timber and that
only the finest mix is used for the outer layer:

C10. MIXING
Where concrete is required for exposed
finished shuttered work, the first mix of
each day shall consist of sand and cement
without the coarse aggregate as specified
and shall be spread lightly upon the bottom
of the formwork in order to avoid the first mix
showing excessive aggregate. (ibid., p.30)

By specifying the finest mix at the surface
of the wall the architect ensures that only
the timber shuttering will determine the
appearance of the concrete. Other aspects of
fabrication and the materiality of the concrete
itself are censored.

The concrete in the external walls of the
Val Harding house is designed to be
seamless and homogeneous. Its shape is
determined through a rigid formwork, which
itself is determined by the techniques of an

7

6

architectural drawing. It is concrete as matter – neutral, without identity, waiting to be given form. The concrete in the assembly hall walls of the Elfrida Rathbone School is mimetic as Barthes has described plastic: it imitates timber. Concrete is treated as matter; it is given form at the scale of the formwork and the building and at the scale of material detail.

The specification for the Elfrida Rathbone School devotes much attention to ensuring that the concrete shows no variation. For example:

C6.
The contractor will reserve sufficient sand and gravel with Messrs. Eastwoods to complete the whole of the exposed shuttered concrete works without undue variation of colour. (ibid., p.26)

C14.
Where concrete beams, slabs, etc. are shown on the drawings to be a shuttered concrete finish, the Contractor's attention is drawn to the very high standard of accuracy, consistency and finish of concrete that will be required. The greatest care will be called for in formwork, mixing and placing of concrete,

positioning of construction joints, removal of shuttering, etc. and the Contractor will be deemed to have allowed for this in his tender. No rubbing down or making good will be allowed after removal of the shuttering to any of these surfaces. The resulting concrete surface is to be free of any honeycombing, cavities, pitting and any imperfections not the result of the texture of the concrete. (ibid. p.31)

What is at stake in this denial of variation? On the one hand, it is precisely the irregularities in a material's surface, the smudge of condensation on an otherwise perfectly polished mirror or the crack in an otherwise transparent pane of glass, which draw attention to the specific identity of the material. The efforts to make the material consistent make it disappear. On the other hand, there seems to be a desire for complete control over the material, to exclude the possibility that it will bring anything new to the realization of idea into built form.

The fabrication processes that are described in the specifications for these two walls fit the hylomorphic schema very well. They both use a rigid formwork which gives the concrete its form. And although the concrete does have its own individual properties and characteristics these are suppressed in the details of the construction process and the concrete is treated in such a way that it exemplifies an idea of matter in the appearance of the finished walls.

The concrete of Wall One resists description in the terms of the hylomorphic schema. Instead of being designed to present concrete as homogeneous matter this fabrication process allows the variation in the colour and size of aggregate to be visible at the surface. Concrete is revealed as an individual material with its own characteristics in part through the residues of its particular processes of formation. Where, for example, the changes between pours in the Val Harding house were made as seamless as possible through the use of timber stops and removing any excess around them,[5] Wall One is allowed, literally, to come apart at the seams (Figure 6). Where surface irregularities and 'imperfections' were prohibited in the Elfrida Rathbone walls, the sweating in Wall One produces a micro topography of process that is particular to concrete, and to this particular concrete with its high moisture content.

The examples of rigid formwork casting exemplify fabrication in the terms of the form/matter model, and go to great lengths to deny the material variation of concrete and produce it in such a way that it conforms to the idea of 'matter'. For Gilles Deleuze and Félix Guattari, this denial of the active and affective energies and variations of material is inherent to the hylomorphic schema in which matter is homogeneous and inert. With reference to Simondon's critique they explain that:

Simondon exposes the technological insufficiency of the matter–form model, in that it assumes a fixed form and a matter deemed homogeneous … Simondon demonstrates that the hylomorphic model leaves many things, active and affective, by the wayside. On the one hand, to the formed or formable matter we must add an entire energetic materiality in movement, carrying singularities or haecceities that are already like implicit forms that are topological, rather than geometrical, and that combine with processes of deformation: for example the variable undulations and torsions of the fibers guiding the operation of splitting wood. On the other hand we must add variable intensive affects, now resulting from the operation, now on the contrary making it possible: for example, wood that is more or less porous, more or less elastic and resistant. (Deleuze and Guattari 1988, p.408)

In the fabrication of Wall One, the particular mixes of concrete, their actions and interactions at the micro scales of aggregate and water content, and at the macro scale of sinking setting mass are allowed to generate form and to produce variation. The concrete of Wall One emerges, not just as material rather than matter, but as material that is itself variegated and differentiating throughout its mass, that is active, and acts according to these differences and in relation to the materials and forces it is in contact with. Wall One demands an alternative account of materials as active, intensive and heterogeneous. The simple imposition of form on matter is no adequate description.

Imposing form: hierarchies and forces in concrete casting

When I see the rig itself – which Alan calls a 'jig', 'a device for holding a piece to be worked, rather than a means of predetermining the piece exactly'[6] – it resembles a diagram of forces. A timber skeleton with panelled sides and a heavy top which is free to slide up and down is reinforced vertically by some acro props – ready made columns. Between the top rail and the base are threaded steel cables which can be tightened. This adjustable corset will squeeze and hold the weight of the liquid concrete when it is poured into its black breathing skin. Working swiftly, collectively, at the pace of the setting mass, the team of fabricators will push and pull this lattice so that it prevents the concrete from splaying to the ground and performs the miracle of holding it into a standing, undulating curve (See Figures 6,7).

If, on the one hand, the hylomorphic schema renders matter inert and homogeneous, it also ascribes all the potential for action to form which has power over yielding matter and dominates it. A hierarchy is at work in the form/matter schema, which, as Simondon strikingly points out, is also reproduced in social relations:

The technical procedure which imposes a form on a passive and indeterminate matter is not just an abstract procedure witnessed by the spectator who sees what goes in and out of the workshop without knowing the exact process. It is essentially the procedure commanded by the free man and carried out by the slave.[7]

In making this parallel Simondon makes clear the power differential inherent to the hylomorphic schema. And in an extraordinary passage from his introduction to *Political Physics* John Protevi takes this parallel even further and represents Simondon's free man

5

See clauses 133, 'stops', and 134: 'If any concrete flows past the stop, it shall be hacked off as soon as the concrete has congealed', Harding 1934, p.16.

6

Chandler 2004, p.207.

7

Simondon 1964, p.48. My translation with thanks to Tara Delinde for her help with the French.

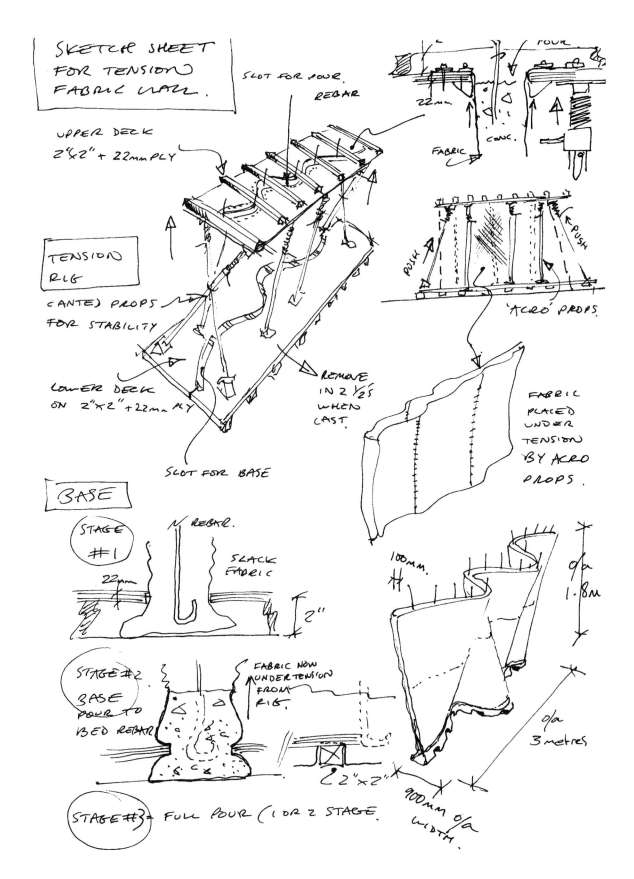

SKETCH SHEET
FOR TENSION
FABRIC WALL.

SLOT FOR POUR.
REBAR

POUR

22mm.

FABRIC   CONC.

UPPER DECK
2"x2" + 22mmPLY

TENSION
RIG

(CANTE) PROPS
FOR STABILITY

PUSH   PUSH

'ACRO' PROPS.

LOWER DECK
ON 2"x2" + 22mm PLY

REMOVE
IN 2 1/2s
WHEN
CAST.

FABRIC
PLACED
UNDER
TENSION
BY ACRO
PROPS.

SLOT FOR BASE

BASE

STAGE
#1

REBAR.

SLACK
FABRIC

22mm

2"

100mm.

o/a
1.8m

STAGE#2
BASE
POUR TO
BED REBAR

FABRIC NOW
UNDER TENSION
FROM
RIG.

2"x2"

o/a
3 metres

STAGE#3- FULL POUR (1 OR 2 STAGE.

900mm o/a
WIDTH.

who imposes form on passive matter, who despises 'surrender' to matter and 'only sees and commands' as an architect (2001, p.4). The architect, in imposing form, treats not only the material but, importantly, the slave who carries out his commands, as if both are passive and will receive his directions accordingly.

The specifications for the two examples of conventionally cast walls show the extent to which the formwork and its related techniques are intended to produce a perfect and fully determined realization of the architect's vision in concrete. They demonstrate what Protevi refers to (using Plato's term) as 'architectonic techne' in which the 'architect' believes himself to be in control both of the production process and of matter itself. We can certainly read the clauses of the specifications for the Val Harding house and the Elfrida Rathbone School in this way. Not only do they describe the objects, they are also a series of instructions for the fabricators which determine precisely their behaviour. Thus the instructions produce not only buildings but the bodies of the workers who carry them out.[8]

In Wall One the hylomorphic hierarchy is undermined. Matter is more than passive; it does not simply surrender and takes an active role in the determination of its form. In addition, the constructors are able to make adjustments to the cables and bolts as they fill the bag with concrete, thus manipulating the form as they build. There is a double letting go: both the architect (the free man) and the means of construction (the slave) relinquish some control over the outcome.

At the most obvious level the use of a flexible rig to make Wall One instead of a rigid formwork already subverts the simple domination of form over matter. The forming of Wall One is an interaction between matter and form – it is only when the concrete is poured into the geotextile bag that it becomes rigid enough to become formwork at all. The cables restrain the concrete, but their position is, in turn, determined by the mass of the concrete. Concrete and rig are in dynamic relation, neither in full control, nor inert. The dominance of matter by form is replaced by interaction, the erasure of process by a choreography of parts which is manifest in the finished object.

At another level the relationships between architect, fabricators, process and material in the making of Wall One do not fit Protevi's vision of production in the social conditions of slave society where:

all production is credited to the direction provided by the eidetic vision and ordering command of the architect/master/ruler. The work of the artisan is unworthy of notice; he only follows orders, merely allows the realization of form in matter. He himself is in

need of direction from above, and the matter with which he works is only a hindrance to the reproduction of form.[9]

In conventional architectural practice, drawings and specifications outline, with varying degrees of precision, not only how the finished piece will be, but how it will be made. While the fabrication process that brings the rigid cast walls into being is almost invisible in the artifacts, it appears in great detail in the set of instructions to the builder. The 'Concretor' section is the longest in the Harding house specification. Over 10,000 words are dedicated to 'Section C' in the Elfrida Rathbone School specification although it is a building which is built predominantly in brick!

Although Alan is still the instigator and designer of Wall One (or at least of the jig), the instructions he gives are not fully prescriptive and the fabricators are encouraged to modify the process that has been envisaged according to how the concrete behaves and to ideas they might have during the construction. The open endedness of the early sketches (Figure 9) and email exchanges between fabric formwork builders is maintained in the fabrication process and translates into what we might understand, using Protevi's term, as an artisanal process of fabrication.

Hylomorphism is a transcendental illusion: the architect arrogating to himself, to his vision of form and his directions for its imposition in formless chaotic matter, all credit for the production which actually occurs through artisanal work with the implicit forms of matter. (2001, p.122)

The idea of the artisanal has a powerful legacy for architects. According to Ruskin, writing in *The Stones of Venice*, we can identify two modes of building. Classical building was 'servile' – the slave carried out the orders of the master – while gothic building was 'Christian' (sometimes described as 'democratic'), where the 'system, in confessing the imperfections of the human soul and bestowing "dignity upon the acknowledgement of unworthiness" gave scope for the workman to do as best he could, *following the dictates of his soul'*(Swenarton 1989, p.24, quoting Ruskin; my italics). Following Ruskin, we could draw the happy conclusion that the makers of Wall One are somehow liberated from slavery, but this would be to ignore two very important points. First, for critics of the form/ matter model, the artisan does not follow 'the dictates of his soul', but the tendencies and forces of the materials he or she works. Deleuze and Guattari, for example, recognize the artisan's following of matter at a number of levels, and refer particularly to the historical figure of the journeyman:

8

This is particularly apparent in the Elfrida Rathbone specification which supplies endless detail about how precisely buckets are to be washed out, or cement is to be measured. This kind of detail is rarely included in contemporary specifications.

9

2001, p.123. Protevi is writing about Plato here and the slave society that he describes is that of the ancient Greeks. Simondon seems to use the term 'slave' (l'esclave) more as an analogy for the (late 1950s) factory worker.

10
Deleuze and Guattari,
op.cit., p.369. See
also Simondon, op.cit.,
p.49. 'The active
nature of form and
the passive nature of
matter correspond to
the conditions a social
hierarchy assumes for
the transmission of
order: it is the continuity
of the order that
suggests that matter
is the indeterminate
factor and the form is
the determinate factor,
logical and expressible.'

11
Following Deleuze and
Guattari again, John
Protevi suggests that
artisans follow the
machinic phylum; they
are 'itinerants', and
he cites Deleuze and
Guattari, A Thousand
Plateaus: 'To follow
the flow of matter is to
itinerate, to ambulate.
It is intuition in action.'
Fn.25, p.206.

12
Email from Remo
Pedreschi to Alan
Chandler, Mark West,
28 January 2004.

13
Email from Mark West
to Alan Chandler, 4
February 2004.

14
Unit Project, AA
Student Forum,
London: AA
Publications, 1993.

[A]n artisan who planes follows the wood, the fibers of the wood, without changing location. But this way of following is only one particular sequence in a more general process. For artisans are obliged to follow in another way as well, in other words, to go find the wood where it lies, and to find the wood with the right kind of fibers … We will therefore define the artisan as one who is determined in such a way to follow the flow of matter, a machinic phylum.(1988, p.409)

Second, it is a mistake to understand the artisanal as an alternative to the hylomorphic. Just as there must always be a dominant

intention in the making of an artifact (for Wall One that intention must be to keep the mass of concrete upright), the material will always provide tendencies and resistances which the fabricator responds to. Even in the two specifications we have been looking at some clauses allow decisions to be left with the builder. For example:

MIXING CONCRETE
125.
The amount of water to be added to the mix shall be the minimum that is required to give a plasticity that will enable the concrete to flow into position. (Harding 1934, p.15)

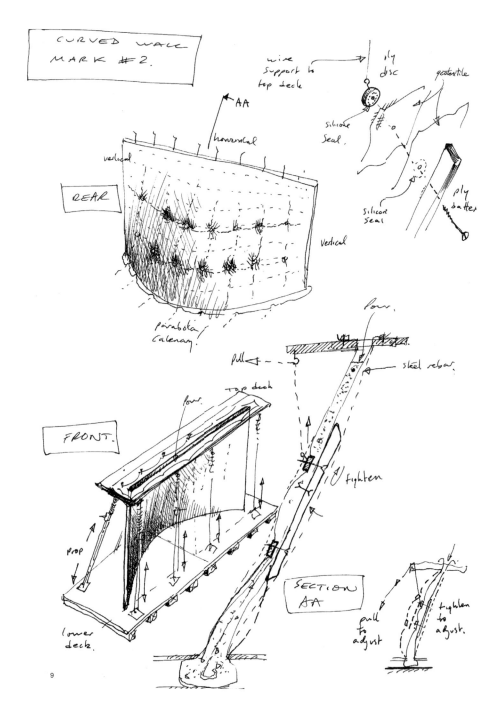

9

C10.
The fine and coarse aggregate and the cement shall be mixed as described for reinforced concrete work above, after which the minimum amount of water shall be added gradually while the mixer is in motion to obtain as stiff a concrete as possible compatible with sufficient workability to enable the concrete to be placed in position in an efficient manner. (Bancroft 1961, p.30)

Simondon's critique is not a Ruskinian cry for a return to pre-industrial techniques of fabrication. It draws our attention to the way in which the hylomorphic schema covers over the complexity of forces at work in any kind of production, and replaces a dynamic network of interactions with a model that is conceived in the terms of 'a society divided into governors and governed and later, intellectuals and manual labor'.[10] Our understanding of production is conditioned by the social context which is already given. Rigid formwork casting sets up a fabrication process in which the domination of matter by form appears to take place. In this way it both attempts to physically reproduce the architect's formal drawings, and to reproduce an inadequate model of fabrication which, for Simondon, 'corresponds to the conditions a social hierarchy assumes for the transmission of order' (p.49, my translation).

Wall One is an expression of the complex of forces which go into its making; their trails are left across its surface: pushing, oozing, restricting, pressing. It is manifestly the result of a series of interactions between a material that is variegated, changing and solidifies in time, between a formwork made up of many parts and between a team of fabricators who bring ideas, drop ideas and make new discoveries about the construction as they construct.[11] Wall One refuses to be understood in the simplistic terms of form dominating matter. Like Simondon's philosophical critique, it questions our assumptions, interrupts an endless reproduction of idea through building and demands a more adequate understanding of fabrication.

Jigging with concrete

In one pile the densely typed pages of the specifications I have been studying, in another the bundle of notes Alan collected in the run up to the making of Wall One: photocopies of product information, chatty emails between experimenters – 'chums',[12] 'friends',[13] – about how best to build this thing, a student project which first used the idea of a jig – 'A jig is a device for holding, an intermediate process between the maker and the made, with a dynamic and consequence of its own'[14] – and his own ink and biro sketches.

Somewhere between working drawings and vector diagrams, they are covered with arrows, dotted lines, questions – 'do we need cables?' – and handwritten instructions – 'pour', 'pull', 'tighten to adjust' (see Figures 8, 9).

For Simondon, a significant problem with hylomorphism as an explanation for how things with an individual identity come into being was that it could only account for form and matter. As Barthes observed of the plastic moulding machine there is only the transformation from one to the other. Adrian Mackenzie summarizes Simondon's concerns:

The basic problem with the hylomorphic scheme is that it only retains the two extreme starting points – a geometrical ideal and formless raw material – of a convergent series of transformations, and ignores the complicated mediations and interactions which culminate in matter-taking-form. (Mackenzie 2002, p.48)

The hylomorphic schema fails to account for the processes through which form and matter interact and bring individual entities into being. For Simondon, the schema:

corresponds to the knowledge of someone who stays outside the workshop and only considers what goes in and comes out. To know the true hylomorphic relation it is not enough to go into the workshop and work with the artisan: one must penetrate the mould itself to follow the physical process of form-taking at different scales. (p.40, my translation)

The first section of Simondon's chapter 'Form and Matter' is indeed a journey into the mould which gives a beautifully detailed account of the formation of a brick. Simondon makes a range of observations which encourage us to see form-taking as a complex of mediations. He lists meticulously all the materials and processes involved in addition to the form and matter, from the sand in which the mould is fired to the moisture which keeps the clay damp. He shows how the clay must be already formed as a substance in order to have the capacity to be shaped by the mould, and describes the micro formations of clay which give it the potential to transform during firing which the unchanging mould does not have. The form is produced, he tells us, by the clay and the worker; all the mould does is set limits to the potential of the transformation.

Although rigid formwork masks the preparatory and intermediate processes of concrete casting, the clauses which specify it reveal a range of preparations and stages involved. In fabric formwork, of course, Barthes' moulding machine is opened up and we are confronted with the complex of mediations and transformations through which a piece of cast concrete takes shape.

10
Deleuze and Guattari, op.cit., p.369. See also Simondon, op.cit., p.49. 'The active nature of form and the passive nature of matter correspond to the conditions a social hierarchy assumes for the transmission of order: it is the continuity of the order that suggests that matter is the indeterminate factor and the form is the determinate factor, logical and expressible.'

11
Following Deleuze and Guattari again, John Protevi suggests that artisans follow the machinic phylum; they are 'itinerants', and he cites Deleuze and Guattari, A Thousand Plateaus: 'To follow the flow of matter is to itinerate, to ambulate. It is intuition in action.' Fn.25, p.206.

12
Email from Remo Pedreschi to Alan Chandler, Mark West, 28 January 2004.

13
Email from Mark West to Alan Chandler, 4 February 2004.

14
Unit Project, AA Student Forum, London: AA Publications, 1993.

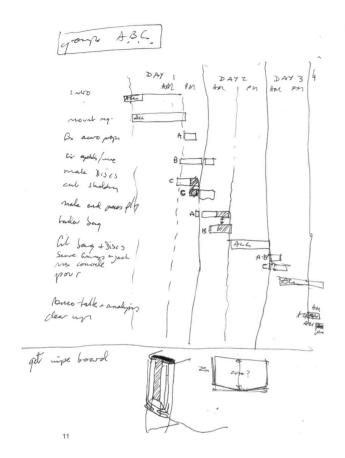

Alan Chandler

From: Remo [R.Pedreschi@ed.ac.uk]
Sent: 06 February 2004 19:17
To: Mark West; Alan Chandler
Subject: Re: Fabric Formwork wall

on 4/2/04 8:33 pm, Mark West at westm@cc.UManitoba.CA wrote:

> Dear Mark and Alan,

I don't have access to a scanner at the moment i'll send a sketch on Monday. I think
that we could use pairs of wires running either side of the gap in the plywood. The
would follow the projected incline of the wall surface. Sequence is important. We
attach the fabric to the underside of the the base plywood and let is lie slack. The
wires or rope are then attached to top and bottom of the the plywood and all the slack
to be taken out of the wires. The fabric is then attached to through the top ply sheet
and pulled tight. The fabric is then seamed at each end. We jack the top sheet up to
pre-tension and then add further pre-tension by drawing each of the two wires across
the wall together using a threaded rod with bolts This could be placed in side a
plastic tube to control the thickness and allow removal.

By inducing a pretension and curvature this way the wire on the front side (as
defined in Alan's sketch) will support the tendency to bulge on the other side.

I would imagine pairs of wire an 50-60 cm spacing. Large ply washers (80mm
diameter) could be used to seal hole around the fabric.

A couple of other details worth think about.

The base of the wall. it the base ply is lifted some 7 cms above the floor then the
fabric can be connected and fixed using 7cm thick battens screwed to the underside. If
these battens more or less continuously round the opening then we don't need to stitch
the fabric on the underside. We have created a a footing for the wall already.

The base ply should be in two halves as this will make it easier to strip and with the
previous point make it easier to remove the fabrics.

Once the fabric has been stretched but before the concrete has been placed the whole
assemblage should be braced diagonally in both directions using vertical and diagonal
timbers. The load from the concrete will be asymmetric and will try to introduce side
sway to the whole assembly.

I've had a wee chat down in our workshop and we are going to do a pilot experiment to
study some of the principles above. It will be about half scale size. It should give
useful insight into the UEL project.

Mark re your visit to edinburgh

What I would like to do with our students is to produce 2-3 very nice examples of
fabric formed concrete that we could then use as demonstration pieces, We have a steel
frame for flat panels and from the above project we will have a steel frame for short
columns and walls. I would like to also include a short beam to show the manipulation
of the cross section. The aim would be to demonstrate the both the pragmatics and the
poetics of the process. The university is building us a a new workshop which will be
ready before you get here and has also agreed to fund an official opening , probably
end of April beginning of May. It would be great to have a number of different
projects on display for the opening.

we should also firm up on your travel arrangements.

Love to Nada and Yesha

Remo

10

In Simondon's terms fabric formwork would be 'metallurgical'. While we can get away with misrepresenting brick making and ceramics through the form/matter model, the processes of metalwork, he suggests, are much more explicit (1964, pp.58–59). As Deleuze and Guattari explain, the metallurgical has the potential to challenge form-taking as a simple interaction between form and matter:

[I]t is as if metal and metallurgy imposed upon and raised to consciousness something that is only hidden or buried in the other matters and operations. The difference is that elsewhere the operations occur between two thresholds, one of which constitutes the matter prepared for the operation, and the other the form to be incarnated (for example, the clay and the mold).[15]

In this sense, then, Wall One is a metallurgical casting. Even the sketches of it reveal it through a series of processes and interactions, as verbs, force vectors and uncertainties. However, in their descriptions Simondon and Deleuze and Guattari focus only on the technical operations and on the dynamics occurring within the material. They

do not consider factors involved in fabrication other than the physical. The specifications for the Elfrida Rathbone School and the Val Harding house do not simply refer to the materials involved but must also detail building standards, suppliers, modes of transport, measuring, the system of checks and authorization and so on. Alan's pile of notes includes the names and phone numbers of possible suppliers, a timetable, a health and safety form that had to be completed to comply with university regulations (Figures 10, 11, 12). The processes of fabrication which are covered over are much more diverse, and stretch out way before and after their time in 'the workshop'.

Following Deleuze and Guattari, Brian Massumi also suggests that we see fabrication as an event occurring between a network of forces (1992, pp.9–20). But his account of a woodworker making a table is particularly interesting because it does not distinguish between physical forces that act on wood (such as the plane smoothing it) and the immaterial forces that produce it (such as the building standard that determined its fire

GENERAL RISK ASSESSMENT RECORD (Form GR01)

Assessment Serial No: .... Date of Assessment
Assessor(s): ....
Location: .Main atrium, AVA building
Signed off by Manager: ....

Work Activity/Operation   **Concrete Wall workshop**

Hazards identified (including estimate of severity)	Groups exposed including numbers and pattern of exposure	Evidence of previous hazardous events	Detail any existing controls in place	Relevant legislation/ standards if known?	Hazard severity HML ?	Likelihood HML ?	RISK HML ?	Additional control measures required (who actioned and by when)	Date Actioned	Date completed & estimate of residual risk	Review date(s) & signature
Injury during formwork erection/ strike	2 staff 10 students	-----------------------	workshop staff in attendance Student workshop inductions.	-----------------------	LOW	LOW	LOW	cordon off area protective footwear/gloves /goggles where required (AC/RL)	29/03/04	02/04/04	22/03/04 [signature]
Use of hand power tools	ditto	ditto	ditto	-----------------------	LOW	LOW	LOW	-----------------------	-----------------------	-----------------------	
Handling bulk materials (sand, aggregate)	ditto	ditto	ditto	-----------------------	LOW	LOW	LOW	staff to demonstrate safe lifting.	29/03/04	02/04/04	
Handling/ mixing cement (serious risk to eyes, irritation to skin/lungs)	ditto	ditto	ditto	-----------------------	MEDIUM	MEDIUM	MEDIUM	goggles/gloves to be worn at all times, masks when mixing dry powder.	29/03/04	02/04/04	
pouring concrete	ditto	ditto	ditto	-----------------------	LOW	LOW	LOW	safe working platform, under staff supervision	29/03/04	02/04/04	

KEY

Likelihood	Hazard Severity	Risk Rating Priority
1. Low (seldom)	1. Slight (less than 3 days off work)	1 – 2 No action/low priority
2. Medium (frequently)	2. Serious (over 3 days off work)	3 – 4 Medium
3. High (certain or near certain)	3. Major (major injury/death)	6 – 9 High priority/urgent action

12

treatment in a certain way). Some of these forces are phylogenetic (the growth of the wood), others institutional (the woodworker's training), others cultural (the form of the table the woodworker brings to the wood). They all come together in the encounter between maker, tool and material. Massumi's account expands Simondon's important notion of the processes that remain hidden through the form/matter model in a way that begins to account for the complexities of architectural production. Architectural practice is never a simple encounter between maker, material and intention, but is always carried out in a context which provides all kinds of 'non-physical' forces – statutory, habitual, economic and cultural – which in turn take part in the pushing and pulling that is the production of form.

If the structure that enables Wall One to be made seems to replace the rigidity and opacity of conventional formwork with an expression of this interplay of forces in acro props, cables, bolts and sliding beams, then the name that Alan gives it seems to give us an appropriate alternative to formwork. It is, he has written, a 'jig', 'a device for holding a piece to be worked, rather than a means of pre-determining the piece exactly' (2004, p.207). That the jig is not fully prescriptive would no doubt please Deleuze and Guattari and Ruskin, for whom the Romanesque arch – only ever the same form – is inferior to the pointed Gothic arch with its potential for infinite variation (Ruskin 1850s, p.167). The jig allows for indeterminacy and the uniqueness of each event of fabrication, but is also a way of describing the complex of forces, physical and non physical, global and local, from within the material and without it, which 'hold' and shape the piece to be worked. Wall One invites us to think of formation, not as the domination of form over matter, but as a jig, enabling a range of forces to act on each other with differing degrees of effect: steel cables, sketches, gravity, school health and safety policy, loose fabric, the geometric concept of a sine curve, someone wanting a cigarette and forgetting to tighten a bolt, and the sluggish, heavy movement of liquid concrete.

fabric formwork

the beautiful, the sublime and the ugly
Ilona Hay

Introduction

Something unusual is happening in the Architectural and Visual Arts (AVA) studio at the University of East London (UEL). Voluptuous curvy walls and fuzzy, hay-like benches divide open plan space. Periodically, smaller scale objects, some resembling knitted curtains and others resembling organic forms, inhabit the space. They have been accumulating over the past few years, a result of ongoing fabric formwork experiments in a series of workshops in the Material Matters and Technology Studio of UEL, run by Alan Chandler.

Chandler's work has been informed in part by the work of Mark West, who also has a history of producing fabric formwork projects. West is the Director of CAST, the Centre for Architectural Structures and Technology, a facility at the University of Manitoba dedicated to exploration of fabric formwork. This facility has access to industrial processes and ability to cast large scale objects. There is a marked difference between his early works, built without an industrial facility, and the ones built later at CAST. They all, like the products of the UEL workshops, have non-rectilinear forms, with curvatures of different extremes. These vary from the subtle bulge to the wildly

undulating. In terms of aesthetic appreciation, there seems to be a threshold between the extremes, a point at which one may cease to admire and appreciate, and instead be awed, or even be disturbed or repulsed. West's body of work contains a wide array of objects that one may classify from the beautiful, to the ugly and the sublime. Examples of these extremes are Bone Beam, which one may consider beautiful, and the Carleton Bulge which may inspires discomfort or even fear, see Figures 1 and 2.

The fabric formed concrete beam dubbed Bone Beam is in the realm of the beautiful. It is a very regular object produced at CAST, where West has been fine tuning techniques of casting pre-tensioned concrete panels and beams, using fabric formwork. Bone Beam has an elegant and simple form, with an evenly graduated bulging ridge in the centre of it, forming the body of the beam. The top is roughly rectilinear. There are regular small 'fins' in the construction, perpendicular to the line of the beam depth. The fins originate partway down the depth of the beam bulge, and finish at the upper edge of the perimeter. Presumably these add to the stability of the beam, but they also add a degree of

Fig 1
Bone Beam, Mark West.

Fig 2
Carleton Bulge
Sculpture, Mark West

1

*Mark West, excerpt
from text from the
Global Holcim Awards
competition entry,
2005-06*

2

According to West,
Our bodies, like those
of other living things,
exist as pressurized
vessels (your blood
pressure; the water in a
vegetable).
This gives us a kind
of 'kinship of form'
with other fluid-filled
membranes, giving
fabric-formed concrete
a deep associative
power; we recognize
these things as
somehow like us – or at
least more like us than
rectangular prisms.
*(West – excerpt from
text from Holcim
Awards competition
entry – date?). Our
appreciation of organic
objects parallels our
appreciation of items
in nature, including
aspects of the human
form. Overstretched
bulges dip into the
less beautiful realm of
organic objects.*

Fig 3
Oxbow Park Sculptures,
Carleton, Canada,
Mark West.

Fig 4
Storefront for Art and
Architecture, New York,
Mark West.

articulation to the object. Along the depth of the beam itself are several regular ripples, probably formed by to stretch within the formwork. This further adds texture to the object. The overall impression is of an object of liquid smoothness that one has the urge to touch or stroke. Its colour, a cool milky white-grey, adds to its allure, and the even light and reflection off its curves can be considered pleasing. This object is part of a body of work moving towards efficiency in form through repetitive testing and tweaking, which yields generally regularised results. Due to the nature of the formwork, there is undulation in the form, but the results are carefully controlled as part of a process of continual fine tuning by CAST. According to West, fabric formwork involves a natural form finding process, paralleling structures found in nature:

Natural structures are fundamentally different from our constructions by virtue of the fact that they are self-assembling (they grow). The geometry produced by the wet concrete + fabric container system does not, of course, 'grow' in any real sense, but it can be said to 'self-assemble' its final geometric form by 'finding' the precise geometries demanded of it by gravity and the laws of nature.[1]

The work of West before CAST, such as the Oxbow Park pieces in Figure 3, are more mannered and sloppy – extreme in form variation. This probably indicates less precise control over the process, prior to using industrial methods. It is more free-form, and artistic – which in itself is not inherently disturbing; however some of the results may be. Many of the works from this period are

quite striking, indeed quite a few are used later as examples of beauty; however some push the limits of the aesthetic spectrum of appreciation. Carleton Bulge, an example of the latter, comprises several overlapping bulges. Its concrete is coarser and darker than Bone Beam. The extent of the swell of the concrete is on or beyond the cusp of pleasing. It can be interpreted as dark, sinister, scary, and earthy or soiled. The overall quality has disturbingly close resemblance to organic objects that we may not wish to have evoked – bulging untoned flesh, excreta, and intestines.[2] West's New York fabric formwork (Figure 4), is also in this category. Carleton Bulge has deep crevasses between bulges. Stretch marks reach from the crevasse towards some of the bulges. To create this appearance, the fabric was tensioned tightly with cable.

Fabric between was left quite slack, so that the void could be overfilled when the concrete was poured. The difference between Carleton Bulge and the Bone Beam can be paralleled to the amount the concrete was allowed to find its own form versus stronger tension or control of the fabric formwork and the concrete. A slightly more taut version of Carleton Bulge, with more gentle swellings, may be more visually acceptable; or, if the articulation was at a very small scale, and was perceived as an even, bumpy, textured surface, it may be considered more beautiful. It, however, is compellingly tactile, and one may be tempted to touch it. Perhaps only one bulge would have been more pleasing, and there are simply too many. Perhaps appreciation of it grows on

3

4

one, as it becomes more familiar, over time, or after further study. It is interesting that it is possible to evoke such a variety of emotional responses with fabric cast pieces.

One may wonder what are the architectural possibilities that result from of the use of fabric formwork, a building process still in its infancy. What are some of the elements required for fabric formed objects to be considered beautiful. Can they be relevant to realised projects outside university walls? And what will the general public think of it? The following examination of the merits of fabric formwork is divided into three sections. The first is a brief examination of a historical treatise on beauty, by Edmund Burke. The second is an in depth review of fabric formwork objects, in terms of beauty. It also includes an updated interpretation of Burke's classifications, discussions of aesthetic appreciation and education, and of aesthetics and the decision making process of casting. The final section examines areas for future exploration within fabric formwork, in the context of aesthetic responsibility. Underlying all this is the question of what shape will fabric formwork take in the future, and how does one judge or appreciate it.

Aesthetics of fabric formwork and Edmund Burke

In order to enter into a discussion regarding the aesthetics fabric formwork objects, it is useful to set out a system of categorisation. Edmund Burke is credited by Harry Francis Mallgrave with charting the direction of British aesthetic theory for the second half of the eighteenth century. His approach is anti-classical; he divorces beauty from proportion, fitness, perfection and virtue. Rather, he defines beauty on the basis of sensations. This is a different perspective to that of that of Continental rationalism at the time. His book brings 'the idea of the "sublime" to aesthetic importance: now a concept having a different yet equal importance to the idea of the "beautiful"' (Mallgrave 2006, pp. 249–250). Regarding his treatise:

The architectural implications, when not explicitly stated, are fully transparent; the architect might in some instances now seek to exploit the emotions of the sublime rather than those of the beautiful. (p.277)

As he comes from a school of thought that is anti-classical, against formal orders, his work is suitable basis for reviewing the beauty of the irregular and non-symmetrical. This seems an appropriate starting point for a

discourse on the relative beauty of objects produced using fabric formwork. His analysis, in *A Philosophical Enquiry into the Origin of our Ideas of the Sublime and the Beautiful,* published in 1757, dissects the experience and appreciation of beauty, and its 'terrifying' counterpart, the sublime. It is a first principles approach to aesthetic appreciation. His is an attempt at a systematic and scientific method of examining the emotions evoked by objects (p.273). His descriptions include an analysis of the experience, both physical and cerebral, of items explored. He attempts to establish standards on taste and passions, and to treat ethics and aesthetics as a science.[3]

According to Burke qualities of beauty include smallness, smoothness, gentle deviation, clarity, lightness and delicateness. He associates beauty with pleasure. Qualities of the sublime include vastness, ruggedness, strong deviation, darkness and gloom, and solidity and massiveness. He associates the sublime with an exhilarating emotion, akin to pain (Mallgrave 2006, p.277). He observes that some qualities of objects may invoke an appreciation of beauty, while others evoke an experience of the sublime. He can not keep the two experiences completely parallel, however, and admits that in some instances both the sublime and the beautiful are united. He qualifies this by noting that the experience when both are united is not as strong to him as when they we apart (Burke 1998, pp.113–114).

Review of fabric formwork qualities

When comparing and observing the two concrete walls in the UEL studio one notices that people gravitate to Wall One more than Wall Two (Figures 5 and 6). Why is this? They were both cast with fabric formwork. Possibly it is because Wall Two has a rougher texture, and is in a more shadowed location. Wall One, the first to be created, perhaps has the energy of an initial sketch. The second, cast to explore a technique, lost some of the freshness of the first in the process. Perhaps it is because Wall One has more variation. Would people touch either of the walls so much if a standard rectilinear shuttering technique was used?

Categories that relate to light, size, variation, delicacy, texture and acoustics are useful to start a discourse of aesthetic comparison of fabric formwork objects. These qualities, discussed in depth below, summarise and amalgamate categories for both beauty and the sublime outlined by Burke.

3
Adam Phillips, from the introduction Edmund Burke's A Philosophical Enquiry into the Origin of Our Ideas of the Sublime and Beautiful, *1998, p.xi.*

6

5

Variation (in form)

The smoothness; … the easy and insensible swell; the variety of the surface, which is never for the smallest space the same; the deceitful maze, through which the unsteady eye slides giddily, without knowing where to fix, or wither it is carried. (ibid., pp.113–114)

This is a – somewhat racey – description of beauty, and one of its requisites, gradual variation. It could easily be used to describe the qualities of Wall One, see Figures 7 and 8; however it is actually Burke's eighteenth-century description of the neck of a beautiful woman. Wall One is evocative of the sensual curvature of the surface of the human body, especially of the female form. It has several visual parallels to the body and its intimate decorations, evoking belly buttons, piercings, soft flesh, gentle swellings and curves. From certain vantages, the view of it can be somehow a guilty pleasure.

Variation is an important factor of aesthetic analysis for Burke. In his descriptions, he clarifies that by variation he means a variation of form. This has a sculptural aspect, in addition to a controlled randomness. Gradual variation is a thing of beauty to him:

But as perfectly beautiful bodies are not composed of angular parts, so their parts never continue long in the same right line. They vary their direction every moment, and they change under the eye by a deviation continually carrying on, but for whose beginning or end you will find it difficult to ascertain a point. (ibid. p.104)

Strong deviation or variation he classifies in the realm of the sublime. Both gradual and strong variation have sculptural aspects to them.

The organic nature of fabric formwork has a certain sculptural element to it, incorporating variation. It expresses a frozen kinetic action, mimicking the force and direction of the fluid within the formwork prior to setting. Fabric formed objects can have the appearance of ice or certain volcanic rocks, both liquids that have solidified. Fabric cast objects are also akin to fossils of plants and animals, petrified organic forms. The fabric acts as a membrane holding a viscous or fluid matter, which parallels the biology of cells. Cells, their walls and their liquid contents, are, literally, the building blocks of nature.

Within nature all material objects can be

Fig 5
Wall One, UEL

Fig 6
Wall Two, UEL

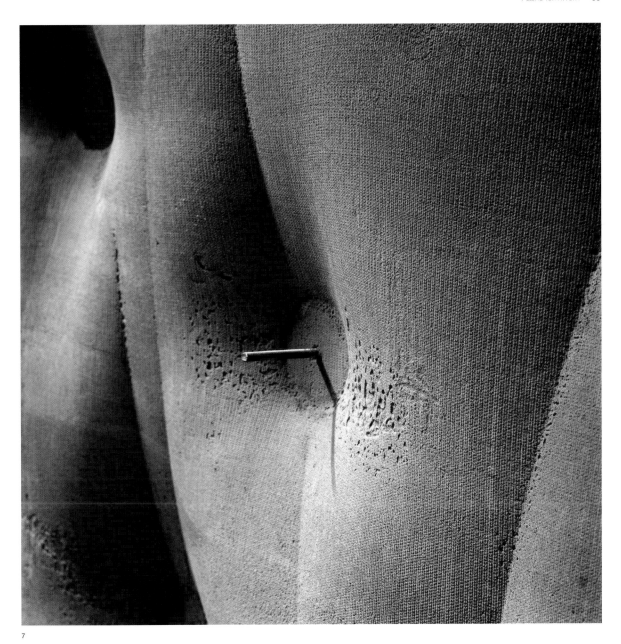

7

considered as structures: the cells, molecules, smaller, and larger units are all subject to external forces. These forces include gravity, air, wind, and water pressure. These same forces act on man made objects. A cell is a hydro, a fluid filled pneu, and a fundamental construction unit of life. A pneu is a membrane separating two media at different pressures. Rigid natural matter, such as shells and skeletons, are hardened pneumatic structures.

Frei Otto's body of work contains many interpretations of natural structures, including explorations of pneus and hydros. Otto's physical testing of natural geometry inspired Wall One. A component of his tensile forms has resulted from research into soap bubbles and pneumatic, air filled structures. Within this realm there is an endless possibility of form, which can be achieved by combining individual shapes, or using cables to create

Fig 7
Wall One, UEL

8

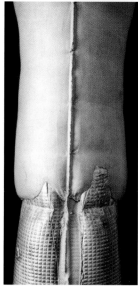

9

10

wais–tlike pinchpoints. Anchor ropes can be added to the interior or exterior, the pressure conditions can be varied, and the membrane can be cut to specific patterns. Parallel form finding methods can be applied to fabric formwork. Means of forming and shaping of objects out of fluid and fabric include cutting shapes with cables and varying the amount, and therefore pressure, of fluid matter against the fabric, see Figure 8. Results of this type of testing of varied forms could be considered grotesque or beautiful, depending on how the material is manipulated by the constructor, and on the viewer's own personal aesthetic sensibilities (Barthel 2005, pp.17, 22 and 28).

Otto also experimented with suspended constructions, and inverting these, which resulted in forms with varying undulating surfaces. Here he is in the company of Robert Hooke, who formulated this principle in 1676, and later Antoni Gaudi, who used this method of form finding for his architecture. With this method, it is possible to transfer the autonomous formation process found in structures in tension, to structures in compression. Very simply, one can dip fabric in plaster, or concrete, and turn it upside down when hardened, to form a dome shape (ibid., pp.24–25).

It should be noted that Otto's shapes are not just form and function:

Frei Otto goes beyond the strict use of form-finding processes and takes a sculptural approach to developing structures. This has nothing to do with biomorphic design; rather, it represents the logical and associative combination of experience with theoretical knowledge and empirical findings.

… [He has an] ability to lend a convincing aesthetic impact to any structure. In his hands, constructions become architecture. (ibid., pp.29–30)

As with the UEL objects, there is a process of decision making that leads to the final expression of form. In the UEL experiments, form finding is immediate, where individuals adjust cables, pressure points, volume as the matter is being cast, in order to achieve a shape. The decisions are tempered by the experience, knowledge and aesthetic sensibility of those doing the casting. The result, it is hoped, is sublime or beautiful.

Texture

Smoothness according to Burke, is 'a quality so essential to beauty, that I do not now recollect any thing beautiful that is not smooth' (p.103). Fabric formed cast objects, especially those cast in concrete with a fine aggregate, retain an extremely accurate imprint of the texture of the formwork, see Figure 9. If a fine grained material is used, the surface can be very smooth. The overall effect, of a subtly textured surface and flowing undulations underneath this surface, as with Wall One, can be paralleled to the beauty Burke found in smooth trees, flowers, streams and landscapes. All these items have a rolling quality, but also a finer textural detail, made up, for example, of individual blades of grass or leaves.

The grain of the fabric of Wall One can be seen, and indeed felt, when one runs one's hands over the surface – and one is tempted to run one's hands over the surface. In some locations, mainly at junctions between one pour and the next, there are imperfections, irregular indentations in the surface, see Figure 10. The appearance of these is akin to that of moth eaten or unravelling fabric, and is somewhat brutalist and mannered. These imperfections indicate where air bubbles have been trapped between fabric and concrete. Smoother surfaces have been achieved where the concrete has been patted, thus agitated, prior to setting. When one backs away from the surface, however, and looks at the piece as a whole, one sees a rolling, undulating wall, and the fine texture is blurred.[4]

Burke further describes smoothness as a principle cause of pleasure in the sense of touch, as it creates no 'violent tension or contraction of the muscular fibres', say, of one's hand, or even one's diaphragm as one tenses with agitation or overt emotion (p.137). Touch and pleasurable texture seem to be items that go hand in hand. Texture, however, encompasses an opposition to smoothness. It can vary from very smooth to something very rough, jagged or brutal in range. When an object is in the latter classification, it delves into the sublime:

A perpendicular has more force in forming the sublime, than an inclined plane; and the effects of a rugged and broken surface seem stronger than where it is smooth and polished. (p.66)

UEL's Rammed Earth Wall has regular, deep vertical indentations that echo the line of timber vertical form supports that held the fabric formwork in place, see Figures 11 and 12. At a large scale, a wall such as this could be categorised as sublime. Regular rhythmic bulges in the rammed earth appear in the horizontal plane. This reflects the process of

11

12

4
A very finely textured surface has been created using a product by Canadian builder Rick Fearn. His company, based in Surrey, British Columbia, is called Fast Foot. The company's product, Fast Tube, is a fabric construction tube, available on the mass market, for creating columns. The finish of the columns created has a regular, even pattern, an imprint of the fabric used to make the columns. Although this is a construction method designed for the mass market – as a cheap and waste reducing way to build – it has a certain aesthetic appeal as a result of the surface finish.

depositing, ramming and bulging that was built up layer upon layer. Rather than reflecting the process of an even liquid that has been poured and has settled into a final form, the matter of which this wall is comprised has a rippled effect which reflects being pounded into place.

The material of Rammed Earth Wall appears rougher than that of Wall One. The variety in grain of the constituent material is more visible than in the concrete piece. In the concrete wall, the finest grains rose to the surface owing to the nature of the concrete fabric casting process; sweating allows water through, but the weave traps cement or sand fines at the surface. In the rammed earth wall, chunks of gravel are visible, and grains of earth vie with the imprint pattern of the fabric. Some locations have rectilinear edges reflecting areas where timber has been used to frame the fabric. And some of these edges are irregular, especially where larger aggregate has fallen out.

Wall Two has an interesting ruggedness, combined with texture, at the corners of the wall where the concrete set in the folds of the fabric formwork, see Figure 13. The dark depths of the folds and their crisp edges create a sublime, jagged surface landscape, which differs dramatically from the even swells of Wall One.

Kenneth Frampton notes the following regarding tactile objects:

[Their] capacity to arouse the impulse to touch returns the architect to the poetics of construction and to the erection of works in which the tectonic value of each component depends on the density of its objecthood. (2006, p.100)

Fig 11
Rammed éarth wall, UEL

Fig 12
Rammed éarth wall, UEL

14

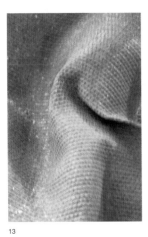

13

Fig 13
Fold in Wall Two, UEL.

Fig 14
Colony, Jane Whitten

Tactile and textured objects encourage one to think about what something is made of and how it might be made, for example out of earth or concrete and formed with fabric. It brings architecture back to the process of building, away from the realm of the image – an aesthetic embraced at UEL. The amount of texture, evenness or jaggedness of a surface can dramatically change the aesthetic perception of an object, whether sublime, beautiful or other.

Size

Size also affects one's response to objects, be it admiration or terror. Generally, Burke grouped small objects with the beautiful and large objects with the sublime (p.103). Perhaps a more accurate observation is the relationship of scale to aesthetic appreciation. What is beautiful at one scale may be considered crude or terrifying at another. Intricate crochet or lacework for example may be considered by some as beautiful, at its normal scale. Canadian Jane Whitten's knitted wool spheres, in Colony, are quite delicate. These have been 'petrified' in sand

in a process similar to concrete, see Figure 14. Colony would have an altogether different quality if scaled up to be the size of the room. The textural aspects and pattern would be interesting, but it would have lost a sense of delicacy. It would be more crude and brutal.

Mass as well as solidity are related to aesthetics of size. Stonehenge is partially appreciated for its size and mass. The mass of the stones and the implied impossibility of the effort required to move them is awe inspiring. However, a scaled down miniature version of this, as illustrated in the cult film Spinal Tap, renders the monument ridiculous. According to Burke:

Stonehenge, neither for its disposition nor ornament, has any thing admirable; but those huge rude masses of stone, set on end, and piled each on the other, turn the mind on the immense force necessary for such a work. (p.71)

Stonehenge is appreciated for its age and circumstance, in addition to size. These ancient, brutal, simple, large, dark, cold monoliths sit in contrast, on a soft, gentle, rolling, green plain. It is an element of Burke's sublime, and a mystery, how such imposing objects came to be in such a place.[5]

The Rammed Earth Wall is more obelisk-like than Wall One. As with Wall One there is a bulge at the base indicating the forces exerted on the wall's material. However, there is less thinning at the top. Overall this wall is thicker than Wall One. This reflects the spatial requirements needed for a person to operate a machine between the two temporary fabric formwork walls, in order to pound the earth down. There are no windows. It feels thicker and thus more massive than Wall One. Overall the wall seems less fluid, for obvious reasons, as rammed earth is not poured. It also does not feel as playful, due to less variation in the form. The result is something more ominous, monolithic and sublime.

Concrete Wall Two was constructed with a very similar formwork to that of the Rammed Earth Wall, and built at the same time. Wall Two has a shape similar to the Rammed Earth Wall, yet has a different quality. It is much less rugged in terms of its texture; however it also has a monolithic feel to it. In Wall Two, the surfaces are smooth and even, and the pattern of the fabric that held the concrete is quite visible up close. The indents of the vertical restraining timber formwork members are more defined than in the Rammed Earth Wall – the two leading edges that pressed into the fabric and liquid concrete are read quite clearly. Also, there are more undulating bulges in a horizontal plane than in the Rammed Earth Wall, which are more pronounced towards the bottom. They remind one of the cumulative mass of a middle aged belly, or of elephant knees. Ripples occur towards the bottom of the wall, adjacent to the vertical timber formwork, where the fabric seems to have strained to accommodate the extra bulge of liquid concrete.

The monolithic nature of fabric cast concrete could be exploited to purposefully create a sublime environment that overwhelms, such as immense vaulted walls and ceilings. This could be used for a new interpretation of a cathedral or basilica. At what point would curvy fluid walls inspire and at what point would they overwhelm?

Philip Johnson, when listing qualities that make a building pleasing to him, includes how cave-like it is, and how it shelters. This implies a requirement for mass and protection in the build-up of the walls, floor and/or ceiling. Another item on his list is how sculptural it is.

15

He classes the pyramids, Stonehenge and 'maybe' the Guggenheim as being sculptural (2006, p.246). His examples, including the cave, have elements of the sublime in them. Fabric formed objects certainly have mass and the scope for enclosing, encompassing and sheltering, as in a cave. There is potential for enclosure in all planes.[6] They could protect those within, but could be daunting to those without. There is no doubt they are sculptural.

Delicacy

The appearance of delicacy, according to Burke, is essential to beauty: 'An air of robustness and strength is very prejudicial to beauty. An appearance of delicacy, and even of fragility, is almost essential to it' (p.105). Delicacy is related to size; something small, delicate and fragile when scaled up can appear sturdy and heavy.

Several interesting small scale formwork experiments have been produced at UEL, including the open weave curtains and cast stockings, see Figures 15 and 16. In these experiments, similarly to Otto's, the fabric is immersed in liquid concrete and then hung to set. The nylon stocking constructions are flexible and surprisingly withstands a lotof movement. In the curtain and stocking experiments fabric forms part of the structure, serving as reinforcement.

In the curtain experiments, fabric is hung in an undulating manner, literally like a curtain, until it sets. The curves increase the integral strength of the objects. The overall effect and pattern in

5

Fabric formed walls, such as Wall Two and the Rammed Earth Wall, could be paralleled to a modern Stonehenge: large freestanding monuments, great in size and mass and with a form that implies the forces that were held back to allow for their creation. There is a real possibility of casting larger, thus more imposing, walls. Fabric formed walls of great scale, though, may require visual relief to break up potential monotony. It is an irony that the ease of their construction contradicts the monolithic visual effect – a relatively light weight material holds back matter simply poured or pumped into place.

6

In a sheltering or domestic application, there is a comfort in the thickness of walls, such as deep adobe, stone or brick walls, with window seats carved out of them. Additionally, the window reveals can be used to reflect light from outside.

Fig 15
Curtain Wall, curtain and concrete sample, UEL

7
*The term delicate
when applied to fabric
formwork surfaces,
however, is obviously
contradictory. With a
very fine grain concrete,
the surface of a finished
piece appears delicate,
if the material that it is
cast in has a fine weave
or texture, the finished
surface mimics that of
the fabric. However, the
concrete object itself
is certainly solid, hard,
robust and strong. It
is possible, then, with
fabric formwork to have
deliberate juxtapositions
of the delicate and the
robust.*

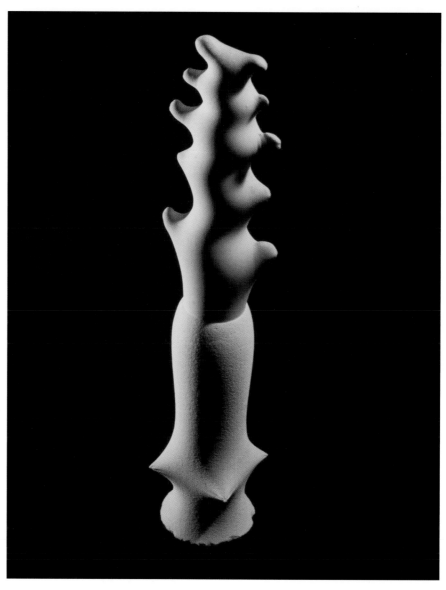

16

Fig 16
Concrete Sculpture,
Mark West

fabrics with very open weaves is akin to that of lace or crochet that has been soaked, then frozen. In these experiments the delicacy of the base texture of the fabric can be expressed.[7]

Light

You can say the light, the giver of all presences, is the maker of a material, and the material was made to cast a shadow, and the shadow belongs to the light. (Louis Kahn 2006, p.236)

Light is a key to architecture, and especially to surfaces that are created with fabric. It reveals the form of the objects in addition to the texture of the surface. Shadows form in unlit hollows of the pieces. There is the possibility within the use of fabric formwork

to create surfaces akin to the fluid forms of virtuoso draperies seen in past masterpieces of sculpture, see Figures 13 and 17.

Burke is certainly aware of the relationship between colour and light, however perhaps not quite in the modern scientific sense: 'All colours depend on light' (p.73). He declares that 'in buildings, when the highest degree of the sublime is intended, the materials [should be] … of sad and fuscous colours, as black, or brown, or deep purple', to create a 'melancholy kind of greatness' (p.75). These darker tones are all within the realm of self coloured concrete, or rammed earth walls.

Indeed, Rammed Earth Wall has an air of sublime foreboding. It has a more ominous air about it than Wall One or Wall Two. This is partially due to its size and shape, but also has something to do with its tone. The base material, constructed out of earth brought from a building site near to the AVA building, is darker than the concrete walls.

According to Burke, in order for light rather than shadow or darkness to be a cause of the sublime, it must overpower, like the light of strong sun or that of lightning. 'But darkness is more productive of sublime ideas than light' (p.73). Absence of light, shadow, can also cause an emotional reaction. With the concrete and rammed earth walls, the darkness and shadow possible can have an earthy quality, with parallels to unlit caves and excavations.

Alternatively, when a dark surface is contrasted with bright light or colour, such as in the shafts of light piercing the thick walls of Le Corbusier's Ronchamp, it can be uplifting, yet imposing and impressive.

Colour, for Burke, can also be a source of beauty: 'Those which seem most appropriated to beauty, are the milder of every sort: light greens; soft blues; weak whites; pink reds; and violets.' Further: 'In a fine complexion, there is not only some variety in the colouring, but the colours, neither the red nor the white are strong and glaring. Besides, they are mixed in such a manner, and with such gradations, that it is impossible to fix the bounds' (p.106).

Wall One has three zones of colour, a subtle tonal change that is stratigraphic in effect. This reflects three different layers of recent history, in this case concrete pours or lifts. The base is one tone of grey and ends at the end of the first pour, the middle layer another tone, and the top yet another. The lighter colours of objects such as Wall One, and the subtle variations between the colour bands, along with the boundary between them, can be considered as beautiful. Subtle tonal variation is possible in rammed earth, as well as in poured objects.

How about fitness for purpose?

Burke, in setting out his parameters for the discussion of beauty, stated that fitness (for purpose) is not a cause of beauty. This is part of his anti-classical stance. He noted that the pig snout, pelican bill, hedgehog quill and elephant trunk are useful and well formed for their purpose but are not beautiful and do not make these animals beautiful.

Many architects today, however, would

disagree. Modernist architecture embraces form and function. Richard Rogers, for example, describes the functional aesthetic intent of his office:

Aesthetically one can do what one likes with technology for it is a tool … To our practice its natural functionalism has an intrinsic beauty. The aesthetic relationship between science and art has been poetically described by Horatio Greenough as: 'Beauty is the promise of function made sensuously pleasing'. (2006, p.252)

Fabric formed objects tend to express how they are made, reflecting forces and imprints that act against them: gravity, formwork holding back fluid matter, volume and mass, and efficiency of form. To some, this capacity to reflect its construction and forces acting upon materials is considered pleasing. Regarding fitness, then, it is useful to diverge from Burke's classifications on beauty and the sublime, when considering fabric formwork. It is still helpful, however, to continue to analyse the objects from a sensory viewpoint, in Burke's manner.

Wall One has indentations where plywood discs, used as part of the formwork, have pressed into the liquid concrete. Threaded rods pierce the centre of the disc-indents. The finished surface has bulged between the fixed control points, but is cut here and there by the wire restraints that held the sturdy geotextile fabric to the discs. The base of the wall bulges, entasis-like in its expression. It reflects the forces of gravity upon the base of the wall, while in its liquid state.

Also in Wall One, the overall combination of a wide base with a more regular pattern, rising to a thin upper portion, creates a balanced effect. The form of the base expresses its role in supporting the structure. The top thinning, to nothing at some points, indicates the minimal load being exerted on it. As seen from the gallery above, the top of the wall is straight and the lower part of the wall curves in two directions, see Figure 18. The two ends bulge in one direction, and the middle in another. This curve reflects the formwork of the base of the wall, intentionally curved to add stability to the structure. Its beautiful undulation has a structural function.

How does such change and variation in opinion regarding fitness and aesthetics come about, between Burke's era and the present day? Education and familiarity have a role in this.

17

Fig 17
Wall One,
from above, UEL.

8

Le Corbusier gives examples of functional items such as grain elevators, aeroplanes, automobiles, cranes, tobacco pipes, engines and ocean liners as architecturally aesthetic. These items are considered beautiful because they are efficient solutions to their respective set of objectives, requirements. They are efficiently engineered solutions. His caption regarding one transatlantic ship is as follows: 'To architects: a beauty of a more technical order. An aesthetic nearer to its real origins.' To him, well engineered forms were both simple and beautiful (1986, p.94).

Education and aesthetic appreciation

Burke explored the role of education in the appreciation of an object. In his discourse on taste, he refers to the 'pleasure of resemblance':

The pleasure of resemblance is that which principally flatters the imagination, all men are nearly equal in this point, as far as their knowledge of the things represented or compared extends. The principle of this knowledge is very much accidental, as it depends upon experience and observation, and not on strength or weakness of any natural faculty; and it is from this difference in knowledge that what we commonly, though with no great exactness, call a difference in Taste proceeds. (p.18)

In other words, one with an untrained eye may appreciate something that one recognises, from experience. Depending on different experiences or backgrounds, one person will have a different taste to another.

It is known that the Taste (whatever it is) is improved exactly as we improve our judgement, by extending our knowledge, by a steady attention to our object, and by frequent exercise. (p.25)

So, as one's experience of an object increases, one's appreciation of that type of object increases. Familiarity with something, or knowledge about it and others like it, serves to increase one's estimation and judgement regarding it and its type. It is a form of aesthetic conditioning, where familiarity and understanding allow a more informed appreciation.

As noted previously, there is now a culture of aesthetic appreciation within architecture of form and function, for example Le Corbusier's appreciation of the simplicity of the form of grain silos, and their expression of their purpose.[8] Their honesty is appreciated. Items that were once considered banal or ugly by people such as Burke, are now hailed by others, who have been trained to appreciate them. Something new and unusual may seem shocking at first but, through time and understanding, may be hailed as beautiful. Preconceptions about beauty are challenged and changed by to this process. Objects can come to be appreciated in a different way, judged via different parameters.

Fabric formed walls, or floors, or ceilings, may be considered unusual as most architectural and building traditions in industrialised countries have evolved as rectilinear form making. This is in part due to the ease of manufacturing rectilinear building materials

in factory conditions. In modern architectural history there has been a multitude of examples of beautiful rectilinear buildings. However, this does not preclude the use of fine examples of curved or sculptural buildings, such as Ronchamp. Over time, preconceptions about rectilinear buildings may even change.

There is a danger of unusual new objects being mere curiosities or novelties. Burke categorises curiosity as the passion of children, and warns that it soon becomes exhausted (p.29). This could be taken as a warning to architects and fabric formwork creators to avoid display for display's sake, to avoid creating objects without depth to them. An element of curiosity in a built object is useful, however, to enable the viewer to want to know and see more. This requires some element of skill on behalf of the designer to create intrigue, and design a building with some depth and integrity. Tools an architect can use to do this include composition, program, tectonics, and history or precedent.

The Decision making process and aesthetic appreciation

During the creation period of fabric formed constructs there is a possibility for controlling their appearance. Their nature allows the creator to make aesthetic choices while the piece is being formed that will affect the final outcome. The creator can thus explore with immediacy. The result of his or her decision can be viewed as soon as the object is set and the formwork removed. Through exploration of form and material, one selects options based on one's feelings and personal aesthetic judgement in a process of selection and rejection. This includes actions and decisions, which can be spontaneous with fabric formwork, such as when to stop the pour, how tightly to bind the fabric together or how much to pound the construction matter.

The UEL experiments are the result of decisions made regarding fabric type, aggregates and media, reinforcement and tensioning of fabric. Decisions regarding all of these have a visible expression in the object to a greater or lesser degree. An element of the hand of the creator is seen in the final product. The composition of windows in the façade of Wall One is an example of this. Their location and size was decided between pours, see Figures 19 and 20. The round openings were created by squeezing the gap within the fabric formwork down to nothing, between plywood elements of the formwork during one pour. One opening, done in the last pour, is more or less rectilinear in contrast to the other curved and round elements of the wall. Some

18

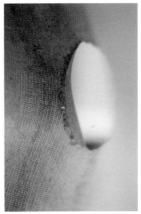

19

of the disc imprints at the upper levels are larger, indicating experimentation during the last stages. The resultant whole is somehow harmonious, but has come out of a random process controlled by the constructors. The product of this group of decisions is pleasing, but in another such experiment the result of different decisions may not be. The responsibility for this lies with the creators.

Areas of future exploration

Experiments in fabric formwork at UEL and CAST thus far are of parts, not a whole. It may be argued that Wall One or the Bone Beam are beautiful as objects in a space, but how could these be realised in buildings? It is now up to architects and building professionals to find ways to make these individual experiments work as a larger whole, and bring them into the realm of built architecture. The future lies in the hands of those building

and developing the construction process and product. Variables involved, discussed below, are statutory regulations, method of construction, constructors, engineering consultants, textile specialists and even specialists from other fields, such as biology. The key responsibility and challenge, though, is to create fabric formed buildings while maintaining an aesthetic integrity.

Fabric cast elements will require integration with other building components and will need to meet building regulations in the United Kingdom. How would they be attached to other building elements, such as doors and windows, their frames, sills and glazing? How does one attach rectilinear items generally to their irregular forms? New experiments out of CAST include prototypes for columns and pilasters within walls, Bulge Walls, see Figures 21 and 22. These combine fabric casting and traditional planar formwork. The intention is

Fig 18
Wall One concave face

Fig 19
Pinched formwork restraints creating opening, Wall One

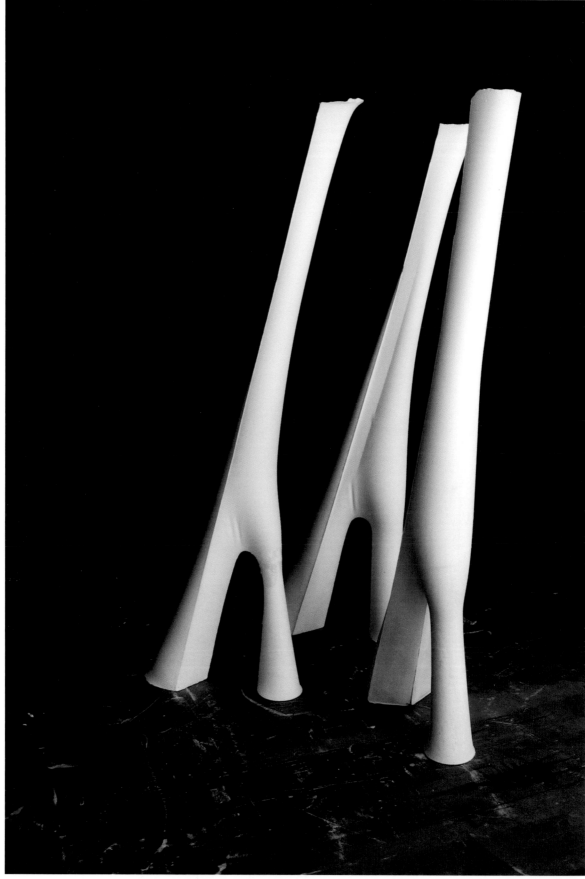

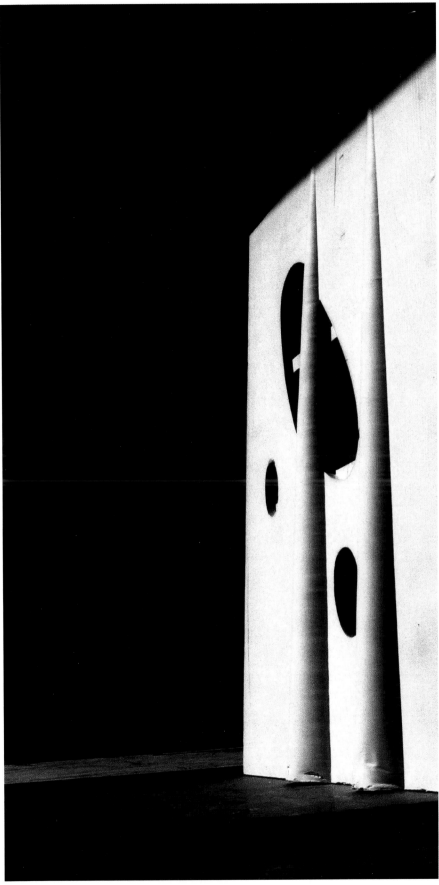

Fig 20
Bulge Wall Columns,
CAST
Fig 21
Bulge Wall, CAST

9

There are already allies in industry. Fabric formwork for foundations, in addition to columns, has been developed by Fab-Form, who promote fabric formwork, noting the reduction in waste and the time required for construction, which ultimately saves money.

that conventional construction methods and tools are used, which makes construction easy for builders. Other experiments in detailing are needed, to create enclosures protected from the elements. The challenge of future detailing is to achieve programme and construction parameters, while maintaining the freshness possible in the fabric casting process.

The one-off fabric formed experiments thus far may be interesting to behold and create, but how are they to be repeated? One route is to complete several prototypes, in order to create items suitable for mass production and for use with standard components found in the construction industry. This can be done via partnerships with industrial fabricators. West continually fine tunes fabric casting in a factory environment, in order to obtain predictable results. Items such as walls, beams, floors and cladding can be precast. Precasting is beneficial in time challenged projects, where objects can be made in advance off site.

Of course, one can cast one-off fabric formed objects on site. Each casting would be subject to site variances. However, it would be possible to base the cast on a specification that has been tested on prototypes elsewhere, for example by students and engineers, or developed in conjunction with associations such as the Concrete Centre. Such a specification could be developed to aid in achieving the appearance required by the designer. The constructor could be left to create the object under their own devices, or this could be combined with site decisions and inspection by architects at key points in the processes. Alternatively, site casting and industrial process can be combined. Industrial products can be developed for use with on site fabric casting, such as Fast Tube, by Canadian Rick Fearn, which is a commercially available fabric tube with which contractors can cast columns.

With fabric formwork, especially site cast, there is the possibility of use by non-skilled labour and scope for constructor expression. This could be a two edged sword: at best pleasant community environments are created, at worst a kitsch decoration. The role of architects and designers in the control, via design, specification, detail or inspection, will influence the outcome.

In addition to constructor and architectural input, there is rich possibility for development with other disciplines such as environmental and structural engineering, and the textile arts. The UEL experiments prove the buildability of fabric casting, but the process is not tested in a strictly scientific manner. The architectural studio provides a safe haven in which to suspend one's disbelief and explore tectonics. It is desirable to maintain the vitality and flow achieved in studio explorations; however, more precise technical research can be arranged in parallel with studio experiments. Ideally, these processes will inform each other.

There is much scope for exploration of services integration. Trevor Butler, an engineer at Building Design Partnership (BDP), London, is currently investigating possibilities of exploiting the thermal properties of fabric formed concrete. There is potential for using the slabs or walls as a heat source, and ducting through them. There is also potential for research in the field of acoustics.

Regarding structural engineering, it is now possible, through computer modelling, to analyse complex geometries and design structural solutions. Peter Rice, engineer at Ove Arup & Partners, noted that the architect's role is mainly creative while the engineer's is inventive. His views and description below are strikingly relevant to the design of fabric formed objects:

This is the positive role for the engineers' genius and skill: to use their understanding of materials and structure to make real the presence of the materials in use in the building, so that people warm to them, want to touch them, feel a sense of the material itself and of the people who made and designed it. To do this we have to avoid the worst excesses of the industrial hegemony, to maintain the feeling that it was the designer, and not industry and its available options, that decided, is one essential ingredient of seeking a tactile, trace de le main solution. (2006, p.260)

He also believes that engineers should aim to control and tame industry. As an untested new process, fabric formwork will be questioned in terms of efficiency and cost. Engineers can aid in justifying and substantiating the value of the formwork.[9]

In terms of textiles, there is further fabric exploration to be done. Fabric types can be explored for their differing properties. Some fabrics may be more useful for leaving in situ as reinforcement, for example. Or an open weave fabric within the wall could serve as a screen. Texture and fabric selection will be based on aesthetic judgement, in addition to structural qualities and environmental requirements.

Textile techniques of pattern making and cloth cutting could be applied to fabric used as formwork, in order to create more efficient structures, or more interesting forms. Examination of textile cutting and assembling techniques – from both the world of tensile structures and the world of tailoring – which involve creating complex forms out of flat materials, could be applied to creating fabric formwork. Specialist computer programs are available to aid in this process. From the realm of textile surface design, printing and wallpaper design can be explored. These can incorporate very complex graphics that repeat and interlock – perhaps useful for arrangement of textured pre-cast concrete cladding.

In addition to precedents in the world of fabric, there is a wealth of precedents within nature to explore, whose forms have been fine tuned over millennia. For example, the structure in the forms and patterns of the shells of creatures such as sand dollars, sea urchins and coral hold exciting potential, and could be translated into the built environment. Their application will require crossovers from disciplines such as textiles, structures, biology and botany. Regarding this exploration, advice from Frei Otto should be heeded:

It is extremely difficult to apply self-forming processes for architectural design. Although [such experiments constitute] … a very direct way of achieving the form, which, by its very nature, has already undergone an optimization process, design work can only be seen in relation to the complexity of a building task and the integration of the building into its surroundings and into society.[10]

Ultimately, when fabric formwork elements are combined to form a building, care should be taken to create an architectural expression that addresses the brief and the immediate environment, and that is also aesthetically pleasing.

Conclusion

A key to the future use of fabric formwork, in the world beyond university walls is to find a way to express its beauty to would be clients, and to reassure constructors as to its validity as a construction technique. Rich potential exists for application of this process in the creation of exciting, emotionally uplifting buildings.

There is a danger, as with any new technology or method, that it may be abused. Its integrity as an architectural element or form must not be undermined by a lack of understanding or appreciation of its intended purpose – it must not be a window dressing. Architects and construction professionals have a responsibility to ensure that buildings are welcomed and enjoyed by their users, be they inspiring, beautiful or sublime forms.

There are several tools that enable one to manipulate the aesthetics of an object.

Originally identified by Burke, but reinterpreted here, applicable qualities that define the aesthetics of fabric formed objects include: variation, texture, size, delicacy and, light. These qualities are part of a palette that architects may use to create pleasing buildings. They encompass the sensuous tactile and visual aspects of fabric formwork. Diverging from Burke, but useful for modern architectural manipulation, the expression in the fabric formed object of the forces acting on the formwork, its fitness, can be used in aesthetic expression.

Architects using fabric formwork within their designs are morally accountable for educating the public regarding its aesthetic potential: early applications will affect the public's future appreciation. Education can affect appreciation of an object: the more one knows or understands about something, the more one may come to esteem it. The more the public learn about fabric formed objects, the more they may understand them aesthetically and view them as beautiful or sublime. This will depend on the quality and beauty of the objects produced. The more beautiful fabric formed objects that are created, the better – this can only aid in their public appreciation.

With fabric formwork, there is the possibility of a close connection between the hand of the maker and the final product. This creates a tactile object which reflects its material inputs. The connection between the material, the maker and the user can be facilitated by engineers and architects alike.

The shape of the future of fabric formed architecture depends on effective collaborations across multiple disciplines, which should address aesthetic, environmental and social issues. The realisation of beautiful objects, from prototype to building, is a key responsibility towards this end.

10
Quoted in Barthel 2005, p.18.

Some technical aspects of the use of fabric formwork

Daniel S.H. Lee

Introduction

Concrete is one of the most widely used building materials in contemporary architecture and construction. It is a material under constant research, evaluation and development. Most often research is carried across a variety of fields, each one largely independent of the other:

> material properties of concrete:
  - in its fresh state, its workability and curing
  - the constituent materials, fine and coarse aggregates
  - the physical properties of hardened concrete, strength, durability, fire resistance

> structural behaviour of reinforced and pre-stressed concrete

> construction process
  - improving efficiency of the construction process
  - new methods of economic design and utilisation of formwork

> architectural concrete
  - finishes
  - weathering

Research in the above areas is often compartmented with specific sub-disciplines, such as the material scientist, the structural engineer, the builder and the architect. The use of fabric as formwork for concrete raises issues that cut across the list and suggest a holistic approach to its study and evaluation. This chapter brings together some of the important technical issues raised by the use of fabric formwork.

The use of concrete is ubiquitous; applications can be found in almost every part of the world as it is versatile, durable and cost-effective. It can be appropriately low-tech or extremely sophisticated. Inevitably concrete is also being studied more carefully for its environmental impact. For example, pulverised fuel ash, (PFA), a byproduct of coal-fired power plant, is being used to replace up to 40 per cent of cement in concrete mixes (Oner et al. 2005). The replacement of Portland cement with PFA reduces greenhouse gas emissions in the production of concrete and reduces the waste sent to landfill.

Exposed concrete structure can utilise the thermal mass to save energy. Concrete has the ability to absorb heat slowly and release it back into the surrounding environment. It can be used as part of the passive heating and cooling strategy of a building. According to

1

*Blow holes are surface defects
and blemishes left by pockets
of air trapped during casting.*

2

www.fab-form.com/

the British Cement Association (BCA), 90 per cent of the total energy used in buildings is produced from cooling, heating and lighting; the damping and lag effect of thermal mass reduces the temperature fluctuations and can reduce carbon dioxide emissions by up to 50 per cent (British Cement Association 2001).

However there have been some aspects of cast concrete that have dogged its acceptance and now require further research and development. The presence of blow holes on the finished surface of concrete is one of them.[1] In most cases the presence of blow holes on a concrete surface is a visual concern, but it may also affect the strength, durability and service life of the concrete.

Another aspect is related to excess water added in the concrete mix to achieve the optimum workability and placing. The excess water is necessary for the fresh concrete to flow around the reinforcement. However as the ratio of water to cement in the concrete mix increases the concrete strength reduces (the optimum water/cement ratio is 0.40 or lower) (Kosmatka and Panarese 1990). Thus it is more desirable to have as little water as possible in the mix, while achieving the minimum workability required.

These aspects of concrete can be improved by using permeable formwork in the casting process. The most significant advantage of using permeable formwork is that it allows the trapped air bubbles and excess water to pass through it, leaving a smooth and denser finished surface of cast concrete. This results in a more durable concrete with higher visual

satisfaction in terms of its surface quality. However the early permeable formwork (conventional timber or steel formwork with absorptive form liner covering the inner surface) was estimated to be 3.5 to 4.5 times the cost of conventional formwork (Reddi 1992).

Use of fabric formwork in the construction industry

Fabric formwork has been in use since the 1950s. Some early buildings of Félix Candela, famous for the design and construction of reinforced concrete shells, were constructed of burlap fabric draped between simple timber arches to create anti-clastic shapes. As the concrete was placed the fabric sagged between the timber forms to produce a ribbed, parabolic shell. The system was used to build low-cost school buildings in Mexico. During the 1960s and 1970s, the Spanish architect Miguel Fisac employed flexible plastic sheets (which were not permeable) to cast architectural wall panels (Fisac 2003). Fisac used the technique primarily for architectural expression in a variety of buildings such as the Oficinas de la Caja del Mediterráneo and the Centro Social de Los Hermanas Hospitarias.

The use of fabric formwork has considerably advanced from these early applications. Fast Foot industries in Canada are marketing a range of fabric formwork systems for cylindrical columns and footings. These systems are promoted as economic and pragmatic construction.[2]

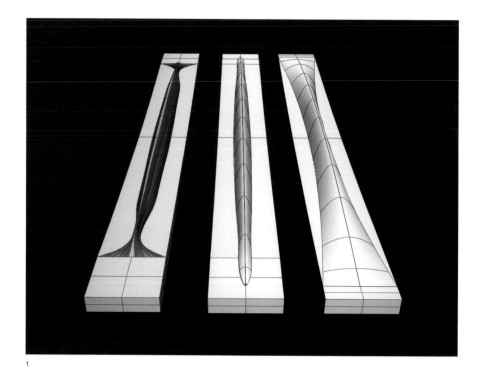

Fig 1
A flat sheet of fabric can be used to form two different geometries of beam

Fig 2
Conventional beam formwork and fabric formwork

1

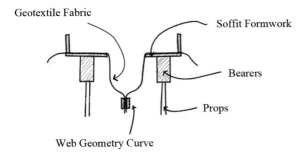

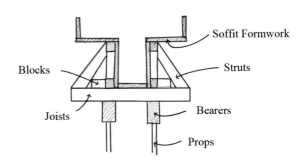

2

Using fabric formwork in concrete construction can bring a number of advantages:

> Fabric is a lightweight, low cost material, readily available worldwide, and many types of fabric can be used. Because of its lightweight nature, it allows significant savings for storage and transportation. Particularly when the formwork needs to be manufactured abroad and shipped to the site, the material's flexibility allows it to be compacted into very small volume, which can easily be shipped by air.

> The effect of fabric on the finished quality of concrete is also an attractive aspect. The permeable membrane of fabric acts as a filter allowing any air bubbles and excess water in the concrete mix to escape. Filtering excess water through the membrane results in a better water–cement ratio of the concrete mix, providing stronger concrete.

> One of the most attractive properties of fabric is its flexibility and with the effective use of this property more sophisticated geometries of concrete structure can be achieved. The overall efficiency of the material-use can be increased by placing only the right amount of the material where required, and as a result, the total dead weight of the structure can be reduced. Thus with fabric formwork, more economical and more sustainable concrete can be produced.

> Fabric formwork is reusable; its geometry can also be easily changed to suit other types of element. The same piece of fabric could be used to produce different shapes of element by adjusting the fabric tension and the application of clamps.

Notwithstanding the advantages listed above, the use of fabric as formwork also raises the following concerns:

> Because of its flexibility, it does not provide any protection during curing so the concrete can be damaged. Therefore, care is required until the concrete has hardened.

> Controlling the geometry of fabric requires careful analysis to adjust the tension forces in the fabric to obtain the intended geometry under the hydro static pressure of the fresh concrete.

> There are few guidelines existing on the use of fabric formwork. The initial process of defining the right fabric type and the design methodology of formwork are still being researched. This may appear to be time consuming for particular forms and hence uneconomic, thus designers may be discouraged from adopting the technique. However once the formwork has been produced this can be repeated very quickly and effectively.

Industrial knowledge about the use of fabric formwork is considered to be in its primary growth stage and further research and development are needed to produce generic rules.

Fabric formwork is undoubtedly a very interesting and attractive research field in architectural materials. According to some recent research results have shown that the use of permeable formwork can produce more durable concrete, and can lead to a more sustainable construction.

Improved quality of concrete

The idea of using fabric material for concrete casting that removes air bubbles and excess water originated in the work of John J. Earley in the 1930s (Malone 1999, p.1). Earley manufactured precast architectural facings using dry plaster moulds that absorbed water from the concrete and produced a better surface finish on the ornamental castings than he had been able to obtain with coated forms. In 1938 the Bureau of Reclamation began an intensive programme of research that led to

3

This test is also known as the Schmidt hammer, impact hammer or sclerometer test, and is a non-destructive method of testing concrete. The test is based on the principle that the rebound of an elastic mass depends on the hardness of the surface against which the mass impinges. See Neville and Brooks 1987.

the development of the first type of permeable formwork, referred to as an absorptive form liner (Johnson 1941; Bidel and Blanks 1942).

According to a report by Philip G. Malone (1999), the earliest types of absorptive form liner were made from ground cane, wood pulp and similar materials pressed to 12 mm thick panels. These types of form liner were used in the Kentucky Dam project (Johnson 1941), and the result showed that practically all the blow holes are eliminated. In addition the concrete cast with absorptive form liner has less water absorption and less damage from freezing and thawing compared with concrete surfaces cast against oiled wooden forms.

Malone summarises the research from a number of studies on permeable formwork and physical properties of the cast concrete as follows:

> Properly designed permeable formwork will reduce the water/cement ratio in the concrete immediately behind the formwork after the concrete is placed and vibrated. The change can affect concrete to a depth of 25 to 50 mm.

> The w/c decreases because water drains from the concrete immediately behind the permeable formwork and because fine materials including cement collect in the volume of concrete immediately behind the filter layer in the formwork.

> The ability of the permeable formwork to allow air to pass through it results in the elimination of surface blow holes and reduces crazing.

The decreased water content in the surface concrete results in the production of a stronger, denser surface which leads to:

> increased resistance to freezing and thawing: the extent of the damage to concrete cast in permeable formwork should be less than one-fifth the damage to concrete cast with conventional formwork;

> a reduced rate of surface carbonation: the smoother surface that permeable formwork imparts to the concrete reduces the area in contact with the atmosphere; the increase in density can reduce the rate of diffusion of carbon dioxide into the concrete; and the increased amount of cement in the surface layer can make additional calcium hydroxide available to maintain alkalinity at the surface. The extent of carbonation in concrete cast in permeable formwork should be generally less than 50 per cent of that observed in concrete cast with conventional formwork and exposed to identical conditions of weathering;

> a reduced rate of chloride ion infiltration: resistance to chloride ion infiltration is extremely important to the service life of steel-reinforced concrete because the chloride ion greatly accelerates the rate of corrosion of the steel reinforcement. The extent of chloride ion infiltration in concrete cast in permeable formwork should be less than 67 per cent and generally less than 60 per cent of that observed in concrete cast with conventional formwork;

> increased surface strength: surface strength measurement methods, such as rebound hammer[3] and pin penetration tests, have typically been useful in estimating the change in the overall strength of concrete as it cures. The rebound hammer readings in concrete cast in permeable formwork should be over 10 per cent higher and possibly as much as 18 per cent higher than those observed in concrete cast with conventional formwork.

The denser surface produced in concrete cast behind permeable formwork makes the concrete less sensitive to poor curing practices.

Marosszeky et al. (1993) also reported an increase of approximately 20 per cent in surface strength in concrete cast against permeable formwork as opposed to conventional formwork.

Permeable formwork will function with almost any concrete mixture, although a high proportion of fines, such as silica fume, in the mixture may cause the filter to become clogged, and reduce the effectiveness of permeable formwork.

Other studies also verify the improvements in compressive strength. Research carried out by Mahdi and Górski (2001) compared the strength of concrete cast in fabric mattresses and cut into 100 mm cubes using an electric saw, with the strength of concrete cast in standard 150 mm steel cube moulds. The results showed that the compressive strength of the cubes cast in fabric mattresses was up to 12 MPa more than the cubes cast in steel moulds. The research also indicated a potential problem with fabrics with large pore sizes. If the pores are large enough there may be a reduction in the compressive strength owing to loss of cement from the mix bleeding directly through the fabric.

Controlling the form

One of the most fascinating advantages of using fabric formwork is to bring sculptural joy into casting concrete. Fresh concrete has

3

the advantage that it is formless and can be moulded into any kind of shape; however, this has been often restrained by the difficulties of making the moulds using rigid materials such as wood and steel. Unlike wood and steel, fabric is a flexible material and proper control of fabric can bring much diversity of geometrical expression to structural elements. Depending on the user, this property of fabric can express the artistic quality of concrete or provide technological enhancement in concrete construction.

Another beneficial aspect of using fabric formwork is the potential material reduction. In the case of a conventional rectangular concrete beam, produced using planar formwork, a large volume of concrete is actually not structurally active. Using fabric formwork can improve efficiency by putting the correct quantity of concrete into the correct place. Studies at the University of Edinburgh help demonstrate this.

The first beam shown in Figure 4 has a web that follows a parabolic curve, the form active

Fig 3
Fabric cast form active beams in the Architecture Department, University of Edinburgh (Lee)

Fig 4
Elevation of form active beams cast in the Architecture Department, University of Edinburgh (Lee)

4

4

Form active structures have geometries that follow the principal lines of structural force. For a beam subject to a uniformly distributed load the shape of the bending moment diagram is parabolic.

5

In most concrete structures the weight of the structure itself forms a significant proportion of the total load for which the structure is designed.

6

For a given geometry of beam and quantity of reinforcement, once the primary steel yields no additional load can be carried. The anchorage failures of the earlier beams were essentially premature failure.

7

www.cdnarchitect.com/asf/ perspectives_sustainibility/ measures_of_sustainablity/ measures_of_sustainablity_ intro.htm

8

The study forms part of the ongoing research programme at the University of Edinburgh.

geometry for a uniformly distributed load;[4] the primary steel reinforcement also follows this profile. Compared with a normal rectangular beam over 30 per cent of concrete is saved, which results in a reduction of the total self-weight. With the reduction in dead weight of the beam there results further reduction in the material use of the supporting structures such as columns and foundations.[5]

Also, a reduction in the self-weight reduces the amount of steel reinforcement needed. A total of nine beams have been constructed and tested to failure. The form and construction details have been modified by a series of progressive improvements. Initial structural failure of the beams occurred at the ends of the beams, caused essentially by failure of steel reinforcement. Modifications to the reinforcement at the ends led to improvement in structural strength although the failure of the end anchorage still occurred. In subsequent beams the form was changed. The flange of the beam was curved upwards on the underside. Thus the flange is thinnest at mid-span and thickest at the support. The additional thickness of concrete at the anchorage increased the strength of the beam such that failure of the anchorage did not occur. The highest failure loads were obtained with these beams, caused by steel reinforcement failure at the mid-span. From a structural point of view this is most satisfactory as it represents the maximum possible load the beam can carry.[6] The geometry of the beam would be very expensive to create using conventional formwork owing to the constantly varying cross section. However, the use of fabric simplifies this considerably. Careful geometric measurements were taken at numerous sections along the beams to check dimensional consistency between casts. All the beams were shown to be very stable geometrically.

Production of concrete with lower environmental impact

Environmental problems are now acknowledged as one of the biggest threats to present societies, and these have led many in the architectural and construction professions toward the idea of 'Sustainable Development'.

Within the United Kingdom, according to The Concrete Centre, just over 100 million tonnes of concrete is used annually. Cement is the most energy intensive component of concrete. If each tonne of concrete consists of 10 per cent cement, then around 10 million tonnes of cement is consumed. One tonne of cement produces one tonne of CO_2. These figures indicate the issue. It becomes imperative to

reduce the total amount of cement produced (and increase the present recycling rate of concrete) in the construction industry as a contribution towards sustainable development.

Embodied energy is a measure of the environmental cost of materials. It is used to describe the negative impact of material production. The concept has been studied for the past several decades by researchers, and it has become a very useful measure of sustainability, although the many analyses are subject to interpretation. Embodied energy is measured as a quantity of non-renewable energy per unit of building material, component or system. The process of calculating embodied energy is complex and involves numerous sources of data.[7]

Research was carried out by Cole and Kernan (1996) using a model based on Canadian construction of a generic three storey office building of 4620 m^2 (50,000 ft^2) with underground parking. Three different construction systems were compared (wood, steel, concrete), and the results showed that the embodied energy of concrete was less than that of steel, but greater than that of timber. In the paper Cole and Kernan state that 'the structure can also be the single largest component of initial embodied energy' and in the case of the office building the 'structure' and 'construction' take about 30 per cent of the average total initial embodied energy. From these statements it can be seen that the reduction of the initial embodied energy in structure and construction plays major part in reducing the environmental impact of buildings.

A study of the embodied energy of the beams described earlier was undertaken and compared with a structurally equivalent rectangular beam. It indicated that the embodied energy of the form active beam is considerably lower than that of the conventional reinforced concrete beam. In terms of the materials themselves – the concrete and the steel reinforcement – the embodied energy of the form active beam is approximately 50 per cent that of the conventional beam. This is due to the reduction in weight of the concrete and more importantly the reduction in the total quantity of reinforcement as shear links are not needed in the form active beam. There was also a reduction in the embodied energy of the formwork itself of 30 per cent.

These figures are indicative and are initial conclusions from an ongoing study.[8]

Additionally, regarding the thermal mass of concrete, the form active beam is a more effective cooling medium than the conventional beam. Jacqueline Glass stated that 'the exposed undersides (soffits) of floor slabs can be coffered or troughed to provide the largest possible "heat exchange" area' (Glass 2001), and thus the three dimensional shape of the form active beam can give a more active heat exchange system with larger cooling capacity.

Using fabric formwork for casting concrete structures is a good response to the concept of sustainable development. The possible reduction in the total volume of concrete used in a structure, for example a reinforced concrete beam, and the further reduction of the material used in the supporting structures such as columns, has already been discussed. In addition, the price of geotextile fabrics on average is about one-tenth of the cost of formwork plywood per unit area, and also many different fabrics can be used and even recycled. Fabric formwork involves cheaper transportation cost owing to its light weight, and most importantly it can produce highly durable concrete with increased service life and lower maintenance effort.

Summary and conclusion

Despite all the above benefits of using fabric formwork, and despite the fact that there are examples showing successful applications of fabric formwork for casting concrete structures, the truth is that it still requires further development for the full technical advantages to be realised. The main research and development areas are:

> controlling fabric geometry and its response to the weight of concrete;

> efficient construction processes for fabric formwork;

> maximising the benefits of fabric formwork guidance to provide the correct material properties of the fabrics themselves (e.g. pore opening size, water absorption, stiffness, adherence to concrete surface) with respect to the resulting quality of cast concrete (e.g. durability, surface hardness, water penetration).

Construction of concrete structures based on engineering design solutions requires a certain degree of accuracy. As stated before, one beneficial aspect of using fabric formwork is that the correct quantity of concrete can be placed in the correct part of the structural element. In order to cast a concrete structure of the intended geometry within the acceptable range of tolerances, careful control of the fabric is necessary during the construction of the formwork, especially when it is of complex form. This is important not only for the accuracy of shape of the cast concrete, but also for the correct positioning of the reinforcement contained within. Research here should involve investigating the methods to tension the fabric effectively, the methods of clamping the fabric and also careful setting of the structural arrangement of the formwork components in order to make the construction cycle (stripping and reassembling) of the formwork more effective.

BIBLIOGRAPHY

Introduction

Nervi, Pier Luigi,
Structures, New York: FW Dodge, 1956.
A translation of *Costruire Correttamente*, Milan:
Ulrico Hoepli,1954

Chapter 1

Alexander, Christopher,
The Timeless Way of Building, New York:
Oxford University Press, 1979

Alexander, Christopher,
The Production of Houses, New York:
Oxford University Press, 1985

Banham, Reyner,
The New Brutalism: ethic or aesthetic? London:
London Architectural Press, 1966

Beer, Stafford,
Designing Freedom, New York:
Wiley, 1974

Castle, Helen,
'Emergence in Architecture', AA files 50, London:
Architectural Association, 2004

Chandler, Alan,
Building Walls: a philosophy of engagement,
London: Cambridge University Press, 2004.
See also *Architectural Research Quarterly* (ARQ) 2004, 8(3/4):
204–214

Christov-Bakargiev, Carolyn,
Arte Povera, London:
Phaidon Press, 1999

Hensel, M., Menges, A and Weinstock, M. (eds),
Emergence: morphogenic design strategies, London:
Wiley London 2004. See also Architectural Design 169

Lloyd Thomas, Katie (ed.),
Material Matters, London:
Routledge, 2006

MARC programme, www.uel.marc.ac.uk/marc/index.htm

Otto, Frei,
'Form Force Mass 5, Experiments',
IL 1990, 25

Otto, Frei,
Lightweight Construction, Natural Design, W. Nerdinger (ed.), Basel:
Birkhauser, 2005

Pedreschi, Remo,
Eladio Dieste, London:
Thomas Telford, 2000

Pye, David,
The Nature and Art of Workmanship, London: Cambridge University
Press, 1968

Salter, Peter, TS, *Intuition and Process*, London:
Architectural Association, 1989

Strauven, Francis, *Aldo Van Eyck: The Shape of Relativity*,
Amsterdam: Architectura & Natura, 1998

Wu, Chiafang and Roe, Stephen, 'What a brick wants to become', AA
files 53, London: Architectural Association, 2005

Chapter 2

Cohen and G. Martin Moeller Jr (eds),
Liquid Stone: new architecture in concrete, New York:
Princeton Architectural Press, 2006, pp.8–19

Dieste, Eladio 'Architecture and Construction', in
Eladio Dieste: Innovation in Structural Art,
Stanford Anderson (ed.),
New York: Princeton Architectural Press, 2004, pp. 182–190

Faber, Colin,
Candela: the shell builder, New York:

Reinhold Publishing, 1963

Huber, Benedikt and Steinegger, J-C. (eds),
Jean Prouvé : Prefabrication, Structures and Elements, London:
Pall Mall Press, 1971

Pedreschi, Remo,
Eladio Dieste: The Engineer's
Contribution to Contemporary Architecture, London:
Thomas Telford, 2000

Picon, Antoine,
'Architecture and the Virtual: Towards a new materiality',
Praxis: Journal of Writing + Building, 2004, 6, pp. 114–121

Picon, Antoine,
'Architecture and Technology: Two centuries of creative tension', in J.L.

Chapter 3

Banham, Reyner,
The New Brutalism: ethic or aesthetic? New York:
Reinhold Publishing, 1966

Bennett, David, The Art of Precast Concrete, Basel: Birkhäuser, 2005

Forty, Adrian, 'The material without a history', in Jean-Louis Cohen and
G. Martin Moeller, Jr (eds), *Liquid Stone: new architecture in concrete*
Basel: Birkhäuser, 2006 p.35

Heinle, Erwin and Bächer, Max, *Building in Visual Concrete* (English
translation), London: Technical Press, 1971

Chapter 4

Architectural Review,
October 1935, pp.123–126

Aristotle,
Metaphysics, trans. H. Lawson-Tancred, London:
Penguin, 1988

Bancroft, John,
*Specification for the Works at the
Elfrida Rathbone School for the Educationally Subnormal*,
RIBA Archives LCC/AD/1, 1961

Bancroft, John,
'Health, Power and Pleasure' in *RIBA Journal*,
April 1973, pp.192–193.

Barthes, Roland,
'Plastic' in *Mythologies*, London:
Vintage, 2000, p.97

Burry, Mark,
Expiatory Church of the Sagrada Familia, London:
Phaidon Press, 1999

Chandler, Alan,
'Building Walls – a philosophy of engagement' in *ARQ*, 2004, 8(3/4):
204–214

De Landa, Manuel,
A Thousand Years of Nonlinear History, New York:
Zone Books, 1997

De Landa, Manuel,
Intensive Science and Virtual Philosophy, London:
Continuum, 2002

Deleuze, Gilles and Guattari, Felix,
A Thousand Plateaus: Capitalism and Schizophrenia, trans.
Brian Massumi, London:
Athlone, 1988

Descartes, René,
Discourse on the Method and Meditations, trans. F.E. Sutcliffe, London:
Penguin, 1968

Gould, Jeremy,
Modern Houses in Britain 1919–1939, London:
Society of Architectural Historians of Great Britain, 1977

Harding, Valentine,
*Specification of Works Required to be done and materials to be used
in connection with erection and completion of a House at Farnham
Common, Near Slough, Bucks, for Valentine Harding, Esq*, RIBA
Archives SaG/17/3, April 1934

Mackenzie, Adrian, *Transductions: Bodies and Machines at Speed*, London: Continuum, 2002

Massumi, Brian, *A User's Guide to Capitalism and Schizophrenia*, Cambridge, MA: The MIT Press, 1992

Otto, Frei and Rausch, Bodo, *Finding Form: towards an architecture of the minimal*, Stuttgart: Edition Axel Menges, 1995

Ovid, *Metamorphoses,* trans. Mary M. Innes, London: Penguin, 1955

Protevi, John, *Political Physics: Deleuze, Derrida and the Body Politic*, London: The Athlone Press, 2001

Ruskin, John, *The Stones of Venice*, ed. J.G. Links, London: Penguin, 2001

Simondon, Gilbert, *L'individu et sa Genèse Physico-Biologique*, Paris: Press Universitaires de France, 1964, pp.58-59

Spuybroek, Lars, *Nox: Machining Architecture*, London: Thames and Hudson, 2004

Swenarton, Mark, *Artisans and Architects*, London: MacMillan Press, 1989

Unit Project, AA Student Forum, London: AA Publications, 1993

Chapter 5

Barthel, Rainer, 'Natural Forms – Architectural Forms', in Winfried Nerdinger (ed.), *Frei Otto Complete Works: Lightweight Construction Natural Design*, Basel: Birkhauser, 2005, pp.16-30

Burke, Edmund, *A Philosophical Enquiry into the Origin of Our Ideas of the Sublime and Beautiful*, Oxford: Oxford University Press, 1998

Frampton, Kenneth, 'Towards a Critical Regionalism: Six Points for an architecture of Resistance', in Charles Jencks and Karl Kropf (eds), *Theories and Manifestoes of Contemporary Architecture*, 2nd edn, Chicester: Wiley-Academy, 2006, pp.97-100

Jencks, Charles and Kropf, Karl (eds), *Theories and Manifestoes of Contemporary Architecture*, 2nd edn, Chichester: Wiley-Academy, 2006

Johnson, Philip, 'What Makes Me Tick', in Charles Jencks and Karl Kropf (eds), *Theories and Manifestoes of Contemporary Architecture*, 2nd edn, Chicester: Wiley-Academy, 2006, pp.246-247

Khan, Louis I., 'Silence and Light', in Charles Jencks and Karl Kropf (eds), *Theories and Manifestoes of Contemporary Architecture*, 2nd edn, Chicester: Wiley-Academy, 2006, pp.236-238

Le Corbusier, *Towards A New Architecture*, trans. Frederick Etchells, New York: Dover Publications,1986

Mallgrave, Harry Francis, *Architectural Theory*, Volume 1, An Anthology from Vitruvius to 1870, Oxford: Blackwell Publishing, 2006

Nerdinger, Winfried (ed.), *Frei Otto, Complete Works: Lightweight Construction Natural Design*, Basel: Birkhauser, 2005

Rice, Peter 'The Role of the Engineer', in Charles Jencks and Karl Kropf (eds), *Theories and Manifestoes of Contemporary Architecture*, 2nd edn, Chicester: Wiley-Academy, 2006, pp.259-260

Rogers, Richard 'Observations in Architecture', in Charles Jencks and Karl Kropf (eds), *Theories and Manifestoes of Contemporary Architecture*, 2nd edn, Chicester: Wiley-Academy, 2006, pp.252-253

Other related:

CAST website, Mark West: www.umanitoba.ca/faculties/architecture/cast/castonline.html

Curtis, William J.R., (ed.), *Le Corbusier: Ideas and Forms*, London: Phaidon, 1999

Fab-Form TM website, Rick Fearn: www.fastfoot.com

Lewis Kausel, Cecilia and Pendleton-Jullian, Ann (eds), *Santiago Calatrava: Conversations with Students,* The MIT Lectures, New York: Princeton Architectural Press, 2002

Oliver, Paul, Dwellings: The Vernacular House Worldwide, London: Phaidon, 2003

Chapter 6

AV Monografias Monographs Issue No. 101 V-VI 2003, 'Miguel Fisac', Calle de Aniceto Marinas, 32 E-28008 Madrid, Spain

Bidel, E.N. and Blanks, R.F., 'Absorptive form lining', *Journal of the American Concrete Institute, Proceedings*, 1942, 13(3): pp.253–268

British Cement Association, 'Fabric Energy Storage – Using concrete structures for enhanced energy efficiency', 2001, 97.383

Cole, R.J. and Kernan, P.C., 'Life-Cycle Energy Use in Office Buildings', *Building and Environment*, 1996, 31(4): pp. 307–317

Glass, J., 'Ecoconcrete: the contribution of cement and concrete to a more sustainable built environment', British Cement Association Publication, 2001, 97.381

Johnson, W.R., 'The use of absorptive wall boards for concrete forms', *Journal of the American Concrete Institute*, 1941, 12(6): 621–630

Kosmatka, S.H. and Panarese, W.C., *Design and Control of Concrete Mixtures*, 13th edn, Skokie, IL: Portland Cement Association, 1990

Mahdi, Al Awwadi Ghaib and Go´rski, Jaroslaw, 'Mechanical properties of concrete cast in fabric formworks', *Cement and Concrete Research*, 2001, 31: 1459–1465

Malone, Philip G., 'Use of permeable formwork in placing and curing concrete', US Army Corps of Engineers, Engineer Research and Development Center, Technical Report SL-99-12, October 1999, p.1.

Marosszeky, M., Chew, M., Arioka, M. and Peck, P., 'Textile form method to improve concrete durability', *Concrete International*, 1993, 15(11): 37–41

Neville, A.M. and Brooks, J.J., *Concrete Technology*, London: Longman Scientific & Technical, 1987

Oner, A., Akyuz, S. and Yildiz, R., 'An experimental study on strength development of concrete containing fly ash and optimum usage of fly ash in concrete', *Cement and Concrete Research*, 2005, 35: 1165–1171

Reddi, S.A., 'Permeable formwork for impermeable concrete', *The Indian Concrete Journal,* 1992, 66: 31–35

PICTURE CREDITS

INDEX